THE CLASSICS
OF WESTERN
SPIRITUALITY

Johannes Tauler

SERMONS

TRANSLATION BY
MARIA SHRADY

INTRODUCTION BY
JOSEF SCHMIDT

PREFACE BY
ALOIS HAAS

PAULIST PRESS
NEW YORK • MAHWAH • TORONTO

Cover Art:
Born and educated in New York, free-lance designer/illustrator ROBERT MANNING
has received numerous commissions for religious theme books. This piece is inspired by
an engraving on the tombstone of Johannes Tauler in Strasbourg, France.

Library of Congress
Catalog Card Number: 85-62399

ISBN: 0-8091-2685-0 (paper)
       0-8091-0357-5 (cloth)

Published by Paulist Press
997 Macarthur Boulevard
Mahwah, New Jersey 07430

Printed and bound in the
United States of America

CONTENTS

CONTENTS

Translator of this Volume

MARIA SHRADY is the wife of the sculptor Frederick Shrady, the mother of six children, and the author of *Come, Southwind*, *In the Spirit of Wonder*, and *Moments of Insight*.

Author of the Introduction

JOSEF SCHMIDT is Associate Professor of German at McGill University in Montreal, Canada. After graduating from the monastery school in Einsiedeln, Switzerland, he studied German, Greek and English in Salonica (Greece), Edinburgh and Zurich where he received his Ph.D. in 1966. Besides publishing numerous articles, he is also the author of several books: one on German Jesuit theater and Jacob Böhme (1967), a standard anthology of sixteenth-century German literature (*Renaissance, Humanismus, Reformation,* [1976]) and a study of Reformation satire (1977). He was the founding president of the Canadian Society for the History of Rhetoric.

Author of the Preface

ALOIS HAAS has been Professor for Older German Literature at the University of Zurich since 1974. Born in Zurich in 1934, Professor Haas studied German Literature, History, and Medieval Culture at Berlin, Paris, Munich, and Zurich where he received his doctorate in 1963. From 1969 to 1971, he taught at McGill University in Canada. Professor Haas has published extensively on Middle High German Literature (e.g., on the Parzifal of Wolfram von Eschenbach), as well as on many aspects of medieval history and spirituality. He is best known, however, for his voluminous writings on the great German mystics of the Middle Ages. These include *Nim din selbes war: Studien zur Lehre von der Selbsterkenntnis bei Meister Eckhart, Johannes Tauler und Heinrich Seuse* (1971); *Sermo mysticus: Studien zu Theologie und Sprache der deutschen Mystik* (1979); and *Geistliches Mittelalter* (1984).

FOREWORD

German is a language for the profundities, and the Sermons of Johannes Tauler are among its noblest monuments. Christina Ebner, a contemporary, spoke of "his fiery tongue that kindled the entire world." Unlike Meister Eckhart, from whom he derives, Tauler possesses a great sobriety even in his most soaring passages. A magnificent C major pervades the Sermons. Long-breathed but urgent, emotional yet firmly controlled, colorful in their imagery, they compel the will to consent. This prose does not date, as does so much of the period. The blend of naivete and gravity gives it a freshness and resilience that has not faded over six hundred years.

To take a purely historical view of this fervent mystic would mean to relegate him to oblivion, to lose sight of what he really was and thought. We enter into Tauler's world when, penetrating beyond the medieval facade, we renew within ourselves the impulses which gave birth to his ideas. He demands that we should understand authentically, that we should not be second hand. What book-learning awakens—and there are numerous passages in which he takes a rather dim view of book-learning—must be freshly tested in the depth of the soul, where after a rigorous process of self-denial our emptiness shall be filled with a new life.

The present translation has been done from the German volume of Dr. Georg Hofmann, whose contemporary version of the Sermons appeared at the six hundredth anniversary of Tauler's death. There are few pleasures comparable to translating an author one venerates. Robert Frost's mot that poetry is that which gets lost in translation has been too meekly accepted. How much poetry gets lost in the King James Version of Psalm 23, or of Job 31–34? Translators should swashbuckle a bit more than they do.

I wish to express my gratitude to Mr. Thomas Sloane for his editorial eagle's eye, and to Dr. John Farina, whose fine gift of gentle harassment has brought this translation to its present size.

PREFACE

Within the three-starred constellation of German mysticism—
Meister Eckhart, Heinrich Seuse and Johannes Tauler—Tauler is
the one who has exercised the greatest influence on the German-
speaking countries as well as on the rest of Europe. It may be said
that his impact on the whole of Europe has not yet found the expression commensurate with its rank.[1] And yet it is evident that Tauler's
Sermons had been circulated in the Rhine and Low Countries, orig-
inally in handwritten, later in printed editions, until they became
practically ubiquitous. Wherever there occurred a spiritual renewal
or a mystical-theological controversy during the seventeenth and
eighteenth centuries, Tauler's Sermons were sure to stand at the center. Since their first printing at Leipzig in 1498, and particularly
since their reprint at Augsburg in 1505—which somehow found
their way into the hands of Martin Luther—Tauler's unique after-
effect within the history of spirituality had been securely established
among the religious denominations of Germany. However, the *"Pie-
tas Tauleriana"* (according to Ahasverus Fritschius, 1676) acquired
genuine international status only when it was translated into Latin
by the Carthusian Laurentius Surius at Cologne in 1548.[2] Surius,
after a number of venomous asides about Luther's predilection for
Tauler, offered his translation to the entire world (*toti orbi*), and it
must be said that he succeeded. It was the Latin rendering which
won Tauler universal acclaim throughout Europe. As happened in
Germany and in the Low Countries, it was now partially retrans-

---

1. The research on Tauler is stagnant in the German-speaking countries. An exception is the research by Louise Gnädinger which brought to light some new aspects: see
"Das Altväterzitat im Predigtwerk J. Taulers," in: *Unterwegs zur Einheit, Festschrift für
Heinrich Stirnimann*, von J. Brantschen and P. Selvatico, eds. (Freiburg/Schweiz, 1980),
253–267; "Der minnende Bernhardus, Seine Reflexe in den Predigten J. Taulers," *Cîteaux*
31 (1980), 387–409; "Der Abgrund ruft den Abgrund, Taulers Predigt *Beati oculi* (V 45),"
in: A. M. Haas/H. Stirnimann, eds., *Das einig Ein, Studien zu Theorie und Sprache der
deutschen Mystik* (Freiburg/Schweiz, 1980), 167–207; "Johannes Tauler von Strassburg,"
in: *Gestalten der Kirchengeschichte*, vol. 4: *Mittelalter II*, von M. Greschat, ed. (Stuttgart,
1983), 176–198 (with valuable references to Tauler's after-effect); *Johannes Tauler*, ed. and
introduced by von L. G. (Olten, 1983).
2. A reprint of this edition: Johannes Tauler, *Opera omnia* (Olms, Hildesheim,
1985).

lated into the various vernaculars. Italy, Spain as well as France received Tauler's work eagerly as a form of *Theologia Mystica seu Affectiva*, precisely as Surius had envisioned it.[3] As a result Tauler—or what passed for Tauler's work, for Surius had included a remarkable number of Pseudo-Tauleriana in his edition—had been drawn into the very center of the Quietistic debate. In 1518 his writings were banned by the Jesuits, and in 1590 the Belgian Capuchins followed suit. Pope Sixtus V went so far as to place them temporarily on the Roman Index, subsequent to their condemnation in Spain.

At this point one may well ask what indeed constitutes the power of attraction which the (authentic) Tauler has exercised to this very day. Surius has hit upon an essential element in the dedicatory preface to his edition. "Tauler's attraction," he says—and he uses very simple language—"lies in the fact that he (who certainly had reached the heights of Christian perfection) never tires to encourage all, as strongly as possible, in the love of God and neighbor; that he exhorts them to eradicate vice, to be attentive to their innermost ground, to strive for virtue and to deny their self-will and inordinate desires; that he invites them to imitate Christ by taking up His Cross and following Him humbly but faithfully in spite of many obstacles and mortifications; until finally the soul becomes so united to Him as to be one spirit with Him, in a most wondrous way. All this is nothing else but loving God with heart and soul and mind, with all one's strength, and one's neighbor as oneself."[4]

Tauler's doctrine does indeed occupy a middle position, which certainly does not signify mediocrity. What it does signify is a "between," an intermediary dimension, which is defended almost with pathos. This dimension is defined above by the most sublime union, below by the utmost deprivation of God.[5] As a result Tauler does not speak from the vantage point of eternity, as does "the noble Master" Eckhart.[6] He takes a position between two extreme points, which are time and eternity. The experience which arises from such

---

3. *Opera omnia*, IIII.

4. *Op. cit.*

5. In respect to this interpretation of Tauler, I would like to refer to: *Herrlichkeit*, III/I: *Im Raum der Metaphysik, Teil II: Neuzeit* (Einsiedeln, 1965), 411–416; *Theodramatik, IV: Das Endspiel* (Einsiedeln, 1983), 407–415. Unfortunately, these editions are somewhat hard to come by.

6. For this and the following quotations from Tauler, I refer to the second edition of von F. Vetter: *Die Predigten Taulers* (Dublin/Zürich, 1968). Hier: V 69, 26ff.

PREFACE

a state is one of anguish: "So this poor man feels as if he were suspended between two walls, as if there were no room for him neither here nor there."[7] Thus suspended between heaven and earth he now experiences sublimity *and* humility, knowledge *and* non-knowledge, security *and* insecurity, peace in spirit but not in nature, imagelessness *and* the world of images. Although this in-between dimension causes grave anguish, it also includes the possibility of breaking through. Faith, hope, and love, above all detachment bring about progress within the two fixed points. Expressed in concrete terms it signifies that "along this narrow path men must take great care to follow the footsteps of Our dear Lord Jesus Christ with firmness and perseverance."[8]

Thus the decisive difference between Tauler and Eckhart has been established. It is the imitation of Christ, placing an emphasis on His humanity never to be abrogated, which makes His passion and suffering the sole model to be followed. Not that the Areopagitic and Neoplatonic language of apophasis is absent in Tauler. However, without shunning ecstasy, it only occupies the rank of an ascending movement toward God, to which corresponds paradoxically a descending movement, marked by humility and self-knowledge, as a concrete force of self-expropriation. Thus this spirituality is characterized by a decisive paradox: it is mysticism of ascent to the same degree as it is mysticism of descent. Knowledge is permeated by non-knowledge. Whoever wishes with St. Paul (2 Cor 3:18) "to be transformed into His very image from glory to glory,"[9] has to undertake the *labor of the night*;[10] light is combined with darkness in such a way that one seems to condition the other. Here we are not dealing with an empty dialectic but with a paradox grounded in the concrete experience of the passion and suffering of Jesus Christ. Accordingly, Tauler knows of no mystical leap from an incarnate to a spiritual Christ, but remarks categorically: "No one can pass beyond the example set to us by Our Lord Jesus Christ."[11] Hence the realization: "The lower the descent, the higher the ascent."[12] Owing to this Christian penetration of the entire Neoplatonic Mysticism of As-

---

7. V 152, 22ff.
8. V 218, 27ff.
9. V 345, 5f.
10. V 345, 12.
11. V 71, 7f.
12. V 206, 4f.

cent, all religious modes and strategies of man have been anticipated and suspended in the concept of God's self-kenosis and incarnation. Fundamentally, Tauler's main concern remains an Areopagitic-Eckhartian *pati Deum* (experience of God by self-surrender) but in the form of a concrete imitation of Christ's humble descent into the world. All his speculative ideas about the innermost ground, sinking into it, returning to it; Tauler's entire doctrine of life and its different stages, stands in the service of a humbling which in regard to Christ is experienced as a lifting up. Thus the experience of the "infinite dissimilarity between man and God" is congruous with that other, which arises from interior discord, allowing the harmony to appear all the more suitable and profound.[13]

It surely was a grotesque mistake—perhaps understandable as a consequence of the religious turmoil which shocked and irritated Christianity in the wake of the Reformation—that Tauler would be misunderstood and misinterpreted as Quietistic. Tauler presents the Christian tradition in its purist form, and the "discernment of spirits"[14] has rarely been so effectively exemplified. For this reason it would be an excellent proposal to question him anew on Christian discernment in the context of a future "ecumenism of mystical experience within the spiritual history of man."[15] Without doubt one will receive answers from him, and although they may not be comfortable, they will have the advantage of truth for the believing Christian. Next to the specifically Christian reference (within the process of the incarnation of Christ), one may also discover other points of departure which would elucidate in what manner and to what extent non-Christian forms of mysticism could be fruitfully employed by Christianity (here one remembers Tauler's Neoplatonic example), or how non-Christian practices of unity could be applicable to Christian ones. Tauler had already been an inspirer among the different denominations over the centuries. Let him now, that the way seems open, become known as a guide across the world-wide sphere of mystical aspiration. His humanity as well as his detachment, which is sheltered within it, qualify him in a unique way.

---

13. V 116, 29ff.
14. V Sermon 43.
15. E. Jungclaussen, *Der Meister in dir, Entdeckung der inneren Welt nach J. Tauler* (Freiburg, 1975), 20.

INTRODUCTION*

References to "German medieval mysticism" usually involve a particular triad in this rich and extensive spiritual tradition: Meister Eckhart (around 1260–1328), Henry Suso (Seuse; 1295–1366), and John Tauler (around 1300–1361), all members of a young and dynamic mendicant order, the Dominicans. Tauler and Seuse were disciples of Meister Eckhart, who died in Avignon facing charges of heresy. Although they were spared the calamity of papal accusation, they did have their share of tribulations in a time unsettled and uprooted by ecclesiastical schism, political upheaval, and profound social change.

Before situating John Tauler in this particular context, however, a few distinguishing points should be mentioned, for each one of these three mystics is distinct in his experiences, his teaching, and what tradition made of him and his works. It can safely be said that Tauler's work—apart from a series of nonauthentic treatises, a collection of some eighty sermons—has found the widest, the most consistent and most continuous favorable reception in Western spirituality. While Eckhart undoubtedly holds the central position in terms of innovative fundamental theology and comprehensive formulation of mystical concepts, Tauler and Seuse were responsible for propagating, and expanding on, a collection of religious insights that, because they had been adversely touched by the odor of heresy, were in danger of becoming obliterated and systematically expurgated, or pushed into the sectarian underground by the persistent suspicions of the institutional Church. Seuse and Tauler were not

---

*I wish to acknowledge with gratitude the helpful criticism of John Hellman and Robert Sullivan.

The following abbreviations will be used with regard to the different editions:

V = Ferdinand Vetter, *Die Predigten Taulers* (Deutsche Texte des Mittelalters XI; Berlin 1910)—the authoritative critical Middle High German edition.

H = Georg Hofmann, *Johannes Tauler, Predigten I, Vollständige Ausgabe*, übertragen von G. H., Einführung von Alois M. Haas (Einsiedeln 1979; 1. Ausg. 1961)—the authoritative translation of the complete sermons into modern German.

(A French translation was done by A. L. Corin, *Sermons de J. Tauler et autres écrits mystiques* . . . (Bibliothèque de la Faculté de Philosophie et Lettres de l'université de Liège XXXIII/XLII; Paris 1924/29).

simply testators of their master's legacy; they developed from disciples into masters in their own right. Tauler's main merit lies in elucidating and transforming mystical concepts of the *vita contemplativa* into the domain of the *vita activa* and *publica*. Seuse, on the other hand, translated Eckhart's mysticism into devotional piety and practice.

The power of Tauler's message in the following centuries is best documented by his reception during the Reformation. In his formative stage, Luther edited three times (1516–1518) what at first he mistakenly believed to be the work of John Tauler (*Theologia Germanica/Deutsch*), heaping effusive praise on this "German Churchfather." The first German Jesuit, Petrus Canisius (1521–1597), author of the *Catechism*, was a young man when he edited Tauler's sermons in 1543. And in the course of the Counter-Reformation, one of Canisius's friends, Laurentius Surius (1523–1578), produced a Latin rendition of the medieval mystic's sermons that finally ensured his recognition as the most influential medieval German mystic.[1] Tauler's role, then, must be seen as equal to that of other great spiritual authors of the fourteenth century such as Richard Rolle or the anonymous author of *The Cloud of Unknowing*. But before we enter a discussion of Tauler's sermons and theology, we will have a brief sketch of his life; even though it is poor in established fact, it is rich in posthumous invention and legend.

LIFE

Very few facts are known about Tauler's life. However, the two major disruptions of fourteenth-century Europe both directly and markedly touched his career and development.[2] The political conflict between state and Church, which resulted in the Avignon exile

---

1. Hans Urs von Balthasar, *Herrlichkeit, Eine theologische Aesthetik* (III,1; Einsiedeln, 1965), 411.

2. For major sources of reference, cf. Bernard McGinn's "Medieval Christianity; An Introduction to the Literature," *Anglican Theological Review* LX,3 (1978), 278ff., particularly IV, History of Theology, 292–299. The same author, together with Edmund Colledge, has translated and introduced the *Meister Eckhart* volume in this Classics of Western Spirituality series (1981); both the introduction and the bibliography contain material directly relevant to this volume.

of the Pope, forced Tauler to spend an extended and formative period of his life away from his native city of Strasbourg. Momentous positive and negative change, disasters such as the outbreak of the plague in 1348–1349 or the famine during the second decade of the century, led members of the emerging burgher class to change their collective attitudes and to turn to a life of spirituality. In Tauler's case it was a regional movement, the "Friends of God," that became the major collective audience of his message. But it is not just the scarcity of factual biographical information that makes it advisable for us to consider his life in the context of general history of the period.

In her colorful historical study *A Distant Mirror: The Calamitous 14th Century*, Barbara W. Tuchman states that the analogies of disaster between the late medieval times and our century are dazzling. The complex disorders "were the hoofprints of more than the four horsemen of St. John's vision, which had now become seven—plague, war, taxes, brigandage, bad government, insurrection, and schism in the Church."[3] But the profound differences between our perceptions and those of that century have to be kept in mind when trying to understand Tauler's spirituality and mysticism:

> Much of the medieval life was supportive because it was lived collectively in infinite numbers of groups, orders, associations, brotherhoods. Never was man less alone. Even in bedrooms married couples often slept in company with their servants and children. Except for hermits and recluses, privacy was unknown.[4]

Tauler was not a hermit; in fact, he lived for most of his life as a mendicant preacher and spiritual director (*lebmeister*) in two very busy towns, Strasbourg and Basle. How then should his mysticism be understood in its historical context? For mystical teaching by its very nature seems to be a private and individualistic undertaking and very inimical to communal settings unless they are of a monastic nature.

John Tauler was born around 1300 into a well-to-do burgher

---

3. (New York, 1979), xiii.
4. Ibid., 39.

family in Strasbourg, a town of about 20,000 inhabitants.[5] The town played a very important role in its region for centuries both as a seat of learning and a center of commerce and trade. The only fact known about Tauler's family is from the circumstances of his death in 1361, during the outbreak of the second (of four) incidents of the plague. He died in the monastery of Saint Nicholas in Undis with his sister, who had become a Dominican nun, at his side. Tauler had begun the normal training of the Dominican Order in 1314, the year of Meister Eckhart's visitation of the Dominicans in Strasbourg; whether he came to know Eckhart in person at that time is unclear. It appears that his status as a disciple of the master's theology and mysticism came through study rather than personal acquaintance. After a one-year novitiate, three years of studying logic, and two years of doing "naturalia" (probably not in Strasbourg, perhaps in Cologne), he returned to his native town for his last two years of studies. During this time he learned Peter Lombard's (d. 1164) *Sentences*, then the standard text for theological studies. His familiarity with Saint Augustine came through the study of Lombard, as is evidenced by numerous references in his sermons. He then was further trained for the preacher's office. The Order's chronicle of the *Scriptores Ordinis Praedicatorum Recensiti*[6] proudly mentions his three main roles as those of a "sublimis et illuminatus theologus, vitaeque magister spiritualis" (spiritual director/*lebmeister*), and preacher of excellence.

The German Dominican Order counted among its members at that time a number of scholars of European renown who were active in the places where Tauler studied. Besides Eckhart the two most

---

5. The most concise recent biographical portrait (with a very informative bibliography) is to be found in Alois M. Haas's introduction to the re-edition of Georg Hofmann's translation of the complete sermons into modern German (1961). Cf. also F.-W. Wentzlaff- Eggebert,*Deutsche Mystik zwischen Mittelalter und Neuzeit: Einheit und Wandlungen ihrer Erscheinungsformen* (3. Aufl.; Berlin, 1969), Kap. III,2, "Tauler," 102–118. Kurt Ruh's article on Tauler in *Dizionario Critico della Letteratura Tedesca*, diretto da Sergio Lupi (vol. 2; Torino, 1976), 1147–1150, is an excellent concise depiction of the man and his work. There is a biographical introduction in English with emphasis on theological questions in the English *Spiritual Conferences by John Tauler o.p.*, translated and edited by Eric Colledge and Sister Mary Jane, o.p. (1961; reprinted Rockford, 1978). For information on the Dominican aspect, cf. William A. Hinnebusch, o.p., *The History of the Dominican Order, Intellectual and Cultural Life to 1500* (vol. 2, New York 1973).

6. I cite the old edition (ed. by Jacob Quetif and Jacob Echard, Paris 1719, 678) since the last volume (T–Z) of Thomas Kaeppeli's modern and annotated edition has not yet appeared.

prominent ones were Nicholas of Strasbourg (*Sermon on the Golden Hill*, 1324) and John of Sterngassen (d. after 1327). Both followed a more traditional scholastic line of spirituality. All three were exemplary in combining Latin erudition with a thorough knowledge of popular devotion in the vernacular.

Strasbourg had seven Dominican nunneries (each having up to one hundred members) and several small communities of Beguins totaling between two hundred and three hundred women. They were, however, not the exclusive audience for Tauler. Given the rhetorical strategy of the sermons, many of them unmistakably reveal Tauler's appeal to several kinds of secular audiences. Through some of the monastic members of his flock, however, we have a few authentic epistolary references. The most notable was the mystic Margareta Ebner (d. 1353), a Dominican nun in the monastery of Medingen (near Dillingen), whom Tauler visted several times. Through the remarks of Ebner's spiritual director, Henry of Nordlingen (d. 1350), we can infer that Tauler soon became widely known outside the narrow confines of Strasbourg and its vicinity.[7]

Tauler was also a friend of the other famous disciple of Eckhart, Henry Suso. Together they established growing reputations as leaders of a group known as the Friends of God, a spiritual movement that evolved in Bavaria, Switzerland, the Rhineland, and the Low Countries. It was comprised of men and women from all ranks of society.[8] They cultivated a life of interior devotion and intense prayer because they felt a need to draw closer together in times of social upheaval. The name, Friends of God, was conceived in accordance with biblical tradition (Epistle of Saint James 2:23 and Saint John 15:14f.; *amicus Dei*). The movement also included a sizable number of Dominican nuns, many of whom enjoyed an intimate union with God in prayer and experienced states of ecstasy. They were instructed by Dominicans. Religiously, the movement of the Friends of God has to be regarded as "an unorganized corporate experience in mystical religion, fed on the intellectual side by Eckhart, on the prophetic visionary side by the older German mysticism."[9]

There is, of course, also a social dimension to this phenomenon.

---

7. Haas, IV,V.
8. Hinnebusch, 320f.
9. Jeanne Ancelet-Hustache, *Master Eckhart and the Rhineland Mystics* (London, 1957), 139.

INTRODUCTION

It was centered in towns, villages, and nunneries. Many of its proponents actually hailed from the emerging burgher class. Tauler seems to have become "the greatest personality" of this movement, "saving it from degenerating into the fanatical extravagancies of many contemporary sects" by maintaining contact with mainstream spiritual Christianity.[10] It is important to keep in mind this role when reading Tauler's sermons, especially when he makes references of this sort (e.g., in the Sermon on the fifth Sunday in Lent, Hofmann [herafter H] 10; see notes for full reference). Repeatedly he stresses his function as a spiritual director (*lebmeister*). He does this to the point of warning against certain intellectual excesses of the academically oriented *lesmeister*, the member responsible for the education of novices.[11]

Tauler often traveled in the vicinity of Strasbourg. But, again, it is hard to discern fact from fiction. Visitations to friends (like Margareta Ebner) seem to have preceded his move to Basle in 1339, which was caused by the struggle between Louis of Bavaria and Pope John XXII. The Pope had placed under Interdict (interdiction to carry on normal sacramental practices) the cities loyal to the secular Emperor, and the Dominicans (and Augustinians), because they sided with the Pope, were obliged to leave the towns that disobeyed the Interdict. During the same year Tauler visited Cologne for unknown reasons, and this seems to have revitalized his study of Eckhartian mysticism. In Basle, where he spent the next four or five years, a period of intensive study and spiritual guidance led to his ever-growing influence among the Friends of God.

Two references make this period significant for his biography. The first is found in his Second Sermon on the Feast of Ascension (H 19), where he refers to human age: "Until a man has reached his fortieth year, he will never attain lasting peace, never be truly formed into God, try as he may. . . . Before the proper time has arrived, he cannot achieve true and perfect peace, nor can he enter into a God- seeing life." Why he would place such emphasis on a period of life that, in the historical context, amounts to very late middle age can be inferred in terms of attaining ascetic tranquillity and harmony or true indifference and detachment. Legend and life, however, illustrate what this meant concretely in his experience. The most

---

10. Underhill, 140.
11. Haas, IIf.

6

beautiful legendary attribution to his life, *The History and Life of the Reverend Doctor John Tauler,* [12] recalls how a mysterious "layman who was rich in God's grace" taught the "Master in Holy Scripture" and true preaching. The layman did this by imposing upon him a prolonged retreat (two years), which enabled him henceforth to dispense divine wisdom to "both the clergy and laity" and become a much sought-after arbiter "in spiritual and temporal affairs." One documented fact throws light on this legendary illumination. The legend was probably inspired—perhaps even written—by a famous spiritual protégé of Tauler's, Rulman Merswin, a wealthy Strasbourg merchant who, in the middle of his life and with the consent of his wife, divested himself of most of his earthly possessions in order to enter truly into the state of a "Friend of God." The record of this conversion seems a good point at which to summarize and characterize the significance of spirituality in Tauler's life from a modern historical perspective.

Tauler's development contained two dynamic components that reflected the dialectics of collective spirituality: the contradiction between humble Christian self-denial and the social individuation that was its inevitable "by-product," and the tension between lay piety and a monastically originated form of ascetic spirituality. One of our most prominent experts on that period, Steven E. Ozment, pointed out the first dilemma in a wider historical context in his study *Mysticism and Dissent: Religious Ideology and Social Protest in the Sixteenth Century;* Tauler and Eckhart are cited as representative figures at the historical root of the problem that fully erupted with the Reformation. [13] But out of historical concern one could also ask in what way Tauler's spirituality was anti-institutional by inextricable logical force, or in fact by an immediate effect of the cause of the disreputable and decrepit state of the institutional Church as revealed by the highest representative. Mystical movements can be regarded as true counter-cultures in that, like official institutions, "they bridge the barriers of sex, age, social class, education and heresy" and as such produce, in relative terms, "democratization" and "egalitarianism." [14]

---

12. Trans. by Susanna Winkworth (same title, London, 1925); preface by Charles Kingsley—in addition to twenty-five sermons.

13. (New Haven and London, 1973).

14. Steven E. Ozment, *The Age of Reform 1250–1550: An Intellectual and Religious History of late Medieval and Reformation Europe* (New Haven and London, 1980), 115.

INTRODUCTION

Undoubtedly, one of the reasons for Tauler's success in propagating German mysticism is his social origin. Firmly rooted in a
prosperous municipality, the imagery of his sermons shows loving
respect for artisans, craftsmen, and farmers without excluding the
aristocracy and its values. And this is surely one of the reasons for
his growing influence through the Renaissance and the Reformation,
and later centuries. His native town was to excel in humanistic learning in a later period (Sebastian Brant, d. 1521) and became the arena
for the most powerful pre-Reformation preacher, Geiler von Kais-
ersberg (d. 1510). The homiletic imagery can also highlight the afore-
mentioned dilemma of individual piety and monastically based
spirituality.

Daniel R. Lesnick, citing the example of the Dominican
preacher Giordano da Pisa in the context of "Religion and Social
Transformation: Popular Preaching in Late-Medieval Florence,"
shows that at the beginning of the fourteenth century Dominicans

> were in fact created by St. Dominic and welcomed by the higher
> orders of urban society as a religious order with the specific aim
> of serving the needs of a newly pre-eminent, mercantile-capitalist
> class . . . a major intention of the Dominicans was to help this
> class as it worked to consolidate its hegemony in the economic,
> social and political worlds—albeit within the context of medieval
> hierarchy—by elaborating an individualistic ideology and for-
> mulating parallel and compelling behavior.[15]

Tauler's sermons, as we will see, are not "mainstream" like those of
Giordano da Pisa. Moreover, this is not the place for generalizations
such as the one above. But the speed with which and the social net-
work through which Tauler's contemporaries adopted his preaching
and his mysticism—the Friends of God exchanged devotional writings in the form of letter references and transcripts—demonstrate
that part of his impact has to be attributed to the social dimensions
of his various roles. As a spiritual director, as a teacher of both his
Order and his town and class, he represented the new spirituality
that developed dialectically parallel to or even away from the monastically based asceticism. It ran parallel to early forms of social in-

---

15. *Europe, Revue d'études interdiscialinaires,* tome 3,1 (1979/80), 19–59; 19.

dividualism while at the same time transcending community-based aspirations and attitudes of a late medieval town and its population.

Of Tauler's many voyages, the most important would have been the visit to John Ruusbroec in Groenendael (Belgium), but we are certain only that another trip, to Cologne in 1346 and to friends in the closer vicinity, interrupted his activity as a spiritual director and preacher. During the first wave of the Black Death he must have lived in Strasbourg. The onslaught of this dramatic event was accompanied by unbalancing social side-effects. The town had its share of flagellant processions—and things worse than that. Even before the plague had reached the town, in early 1549, the Jews of Strasbourg, numbering close to two thousand, were taken to the public burial ground and, if unwilling to convert, burnt at the stake. The town council, which had opposed this measure, was deposed by the guilds and another one elected.[16]

The tombstone of Tauler's grave has been preserved. It shows a slender figure with an open and pensive face.[17] It seems to incorporate the essential features of the actual person: intellectual depth, warmth, moderation, clarity, and mystical spirituality.

SERMONS AND PREACHING

Tauler's legacy, but also his main activity and office, was that of a preacher. There is a social as well as a spiritual dimension to the cultural context out of which his sermons grew.

Probably the most important social factor for German medieval mysticism as a whole was the necessity of providing instruction for the many convents of Dominican nuns. What was essentially an attempt to instill control and order in this constituency, which the institutional Church regarded with suspicion and distrust, resulted in action brought about by the nuns. In 1267, Clement IV officially commanded the Order to provide preachers and confessors for the spiritual welfare of these women. The German province (later divided in 1303) received the practical directive from the provincial Herman Minden (1286–1290) stating that

---

16. Tuchman, 113f.
17. A small reproduction is shown in vol. XIII of the *New Catholic Encyclopedia*, illustrating E. Colledge's article on Tauler on pp. 1944–1945.

9

the word of God should be preached to the sisters "by learned friars in a manner suited to the training of sisters." Consequently the province entrusted its professors with the task of guiding the nuns. These lectors and masters of theology visited the monasteries at regular intervals and, in their conferences and sermons, imparted to the nuns the doctrine that they themselves had learned and expounded in the schools.[18]

The combination of spiritual supervision and instructive preaching is probably best embodied in the person of Humbert of Romans, who served as master general from 1254–1263. During his stewardship, he stabilized the relationship of the Order with Dominican nuns, gave the latter Constitutions, and fended off impositions of the secular clergy. During the last decade of his life, he wrote an important and programmatic homiletic work, *De eruditione praedicatorum* (1266).[19] It is one of a small number of major treatises demonstrating the innovative techniques of preaching in the thirteenth and fourteenth centuries.[20] The innovations consisted of new ways of indexing the materials (e.g., alphabetical or numerical lists of key terms and biblical terms and passages).[21] Also in Humbert's case we have the first systematic listing of different kinds of audiences—a fact indicating the new social reality and awareness the Dominican preacher was facing in late medieval times. Humbert gives clear descriptions and even definitions of the relevant target groups. The Beguines are, for instance, defined as follows:

(Dicuntur Beguinae) quae timore Domini conceperunt spiritum salutarem, et in medio perversae nationis ducunt vitam sanctissimam. (p. 483)

---

18. Hinnebusch, 298.

19. Ibid., 288–292. For a comprehensive survey, cf. Edward Tracy Brett, *Humbert of Romans: His Life and Views of 13th-Century Society* (Studies and Texts 67; Toronto, 1984), chapter 9, 151–166. The *Maxima bibliotheca veterum patrum vol. XXV* (ed. by Margarinus de la Bigne, Lyon 1677) was used since the modern edition by Joseph J. Berthier (Rome, 1898–1899, 2 vols.) does not contain Book II, which is of particular interest in this context.

20. For a representative survey and analysis cf. James J. Murphy, *Rhetoric in the Middle Ages: A History of Rhetorical Theory from St. Augustine to the Renaissance* (Berkeley, Los Angeles, London, 1974). The analysis of key authors of the thirteenth century (like Alan of Lille) commences on p. 310.

21. Richard H. Rouse and Mary A. Rouse, *Preachers, Florilegia and Sermons: Studies on the "Maniaulus Elorum" of Thomas of Ireland* (Toronto, 1979), provide an excellent historical survey in their first chapter, "13th-Century Sermon Aids," 3–42.

INTRODUCTION

(Beguines are women who, out of fear of God, embrace the spirit of salvation, and in the midst of the misfortune of their nation, they lead very holy lives.)

The first part of *De eruditione praedicatorum* is devoted to practical rhetorical advice while the second part (published as *De modo promate cudendi sermones*) provides one hundred skeleton-dispositions of sermons for all classes of listeners, one hundred sketches for all kinds of rhetorical settings and occasions. The thirty-three sermons for liturgical seasons and the twenty-five for feasts of saints are unfortunately appended to only one known manuscript and have not been included in printed versions of the work. It would be wrong, however, to assume that such manuals provided the first real instruction for the medieval preacher. In fact, the sermon in the (German) vernacular was flourishing at that time. Again, one figure may stand for this rich and extensive tradition: Berthold von Regensburg (d. 1272), a Franciscan, whose fame in Southern Germany is widely documented. He practiced a popular kind of homily, addressed straight to the populace at large, and he skillfully married theological instruction with popular forms of devotion.

Tauler's sermons are very often instructions on mysticism; they were not preached exclusively to monastic groups but often show strategies clearly targeted at the secular urban audience of his native city, Basel, or one of the smaller settlements he used to visit.

A more complex dimension of Tauler's sermons lies strictly within the rhetorical realm of the homiletic tradition, for a closer look reveals that Tauler artfully blended the two main forms of sermon prevalent in his day: the homily and the thematic sermon, sometimes preferring one, often mixing them together. Both forms use the biblical quotation as a point of departure. But whereas the *homily* leans toward a loosely structured exegesis of the readings of the particular day's Mass (pericopes), the *thematic sermon* is more a

systematic, logical form of preaching, as opposed to the informality and lack of structure of the homily or of the simple preaching of St. Francis. The theme takes the form of a quotation from Scripture. The preacher then divides the theme into a series of questions which may be as numerous as the number of words in

11

the quotation. He takes up each of these divisions in turn, interpreting them with other quotations from Scripture and applying
them to his congregation.[22]

There is an important underlying feature separating the thematic
sermon from the more open homily: "Thematic preaching is not mis-
sionary preaching. The congregation is assumed to believe in Christ;
the preacher instructs them about the meaning of the Bible, with
particular emphasis on moral action."[23]

Preaching manuals drew on a variety of ancillary techniques in
addition to biblical commentary and scholastic distinctions. The ancient rhetorical tradition as known from Saint Augustine, Boethius,
and Saint Gregory was supplemented by practice used in grammar
and other liberal arts disciplines; the figures of "dilation" and "amplification" used in this development deserve particular mention.[24]
The *thematic sermon* was traditionally associated with the university.
This academic feature expressed itself in the slightly more refined
disposition of the sermon of which Tauler made use in his weightier
statements. The "thema," announced in Latin, was immediately
rendered into German. Often a "prothema" was introduced, amplifying the biblical phrase with parallels from a concordant Scriptural
passage. The "introductio" then save the key concept for the sermon.
This was the place for traditional and catechetic clarifications demonstrating the utility and truth of the thema, if necessary in dialec-
tical form. The divisions used were not necessarily exclusively
intellectual indices; often they served a clearly recognizable mne-
motechnic function so that especially the layperson could understand and retain the form and substance of a given sermon and
reconstruct it for further study. The most widely used amplification
was that of scholastic "distinctions"—these were indications about
the plurality or quality of the material under discussion. Unlike the
division, they did not explain the whole in terms of its various parts.
The "clausio," a summary of both divisions and distinctions, led to
a brief closing prayer or simple supplication. Thus the division (with

---

22. George A. Kennedy, *Classical Rhetoric and Its Christian and Secular Tradition from
Ancient to Modern Times* (Chapel Hill, 1980), 191.

23. Ibid.

24. Lesnick, 34f., gives a concise summary of the standard article on the subject:
"Artes Praedicandi: Contribution a l'histoire de la rhétorique au moyen age," in *Publica-
tions de l'Institut d'Études Medievales d'Ottawa* (vol. VII, Paris & Ottawa, 1936), 111–74.

its own system of subdivisions) and the introduction were the chief persuasive strategies of the preacher.[25] He enjoyed a considerable amount of freedom in leaving out part of this structure or he could use these figures (tropes) to abandon the initial biblical passage and choose a new point of departure—as Tauler frequently did—in the form of a reference from a Church Father or even secular proverbs and statements.

The important status of the mind's disposition versus the rhetorical disposition of the sermon in the eyes of the contemporaries can be deduced from the legendary *History and Life of the Reverend Doctor John Tauler* mentioned earlier. In addition to stressing the conversion aspect of the preacher, the legend also contains in Chapter 4 a "Golden Alphabet," twenty-three programmatic sentences reflecting the systematic refinement in homiletic practice of the past few generations. If one tries theologically to anchor this devout concern about the holy office of preaching, the example of the venerated model, Meister Eckhart, is an obvious choice. The master—some sixty sermons of the many more preserved are judged authentic—had indeed postulated precepts of preaching that would form the framework of the spiritual world he wanted to reveal to his audience:

> Whenever I preach, I usually exhort detachment and that man should free himself of himself and of everything. Secondly, that one should become embedded (*eingebildet*) into the one-fold good that is God. And thirdly, that one should contemplate the great nobility that God has implanted into the soul so that man comes in mysterious ways into God. And fourthly, of the purity of divine nature—of which light be in divine nature, this is truly ineffable.[26]

This is more than a programmatic statement on preaching. Actually it is Eckhart's spiritual doctrine. In order to see that, one just has to compare it with the sober and forthright statement of Alan of Lille

---

25. Besides Murphy, who reviews Richard of Thetford's eight ways of amplification, 326 ff., cf. also Rudolf Cruel, *Geschichte der deutschen Predigt im Mittelalter* (Darmstadt, 1966; 1. Aufl. 1879), 279 and *passim*.

26. I translate directly from the Middle High German quotation in Alois Haas, "Meister Eckharts geistliches Predigtprogramm," in *Freiburger Zeitschrift für Philosophie und Theologie* 29 (1982), 192f.

whose treatise *The Art of Preaching* was penned a good century earlier and served as a role model for later treatises of this kind. He states in the introduction that "preaching is an open and public instruction in faith and behavior whose purpose is the forming of men; it derives from the path of reason and from the fountainhead of 'the authorities.' "[27]

When one tries to situate Tauler's sermons in relation to the master's precepts, parallels with especially the first two points—combining the pastoral concern with the spiritual initiation—are obvious. Tauler's first sermon (H 1, Christmas) is a beautiful example of how Eckhart's first point, detachment, is developed by the disciple into catechetic spirituality. The *Introitus* to the third Mass on Christmas, "Puer natus est"(Is 9:6), starts out as an allegorical interpretation of the threefold birth in which every Christian should rejoice: as a reflection of the Holy Trinity, the true virginity of Mary, and the rebirth in Christ of every Christian. The sermon seems to follow a clear three-point division that is directly related to the theme. But several distinctions lead off the ordinary path of homiletic argumentation into the typical mystical impetus of Eckhart as developed by Tauler. First, the order of points is shifted during the sermon. Second, they are not given equal treatment. And third and most important, the sermon ends in a notion that is not directly related to the biblical theme it purports to teach. Instead, it offers a description of the meaning of silence as a precondition and existential basis for achieving the highest aim that Eckhart considered the first homiletic precept: silence, detachment.

A very astute reader of Tauler's sermons, Martin Luther, was an eager listener for this particular message. Of the few marginal notes on Tauler's sermons, the ones dealing with this particular homily are fairly extensive. This Augustinian monk of the sixteenth century reconstructs without difficulty the distinctions, and he shows familiarity with an Eckhartian counter-theme to the *vita contemplativa*, the position of Martha as opposed to that of Mary (for the medieval master had, in opposition to tradition, favorably compared the industrious Martha to the passive Mary). Luther adds a fairly traditional interpretation according to the four meanings of the Scriptures (literal, allegorical, moral, and anagogical). With uncanny

---

27. Trans. and introduced by Gillian R. Evans (Cistercian Studies 23; Kalamazoo 1981), 16f.

14

affinity his meditation lets him recognize the principal message of Tauler (the notes are scribbled in German and Latin):

> Aug.—got muoss das als ervollen: Vacuum naturale non est possibile, multo minus spirituale est.—Und daumb solt tu schweigen: Silentium Anagogicum . . . Unde totus iste sermo procedit ex theologia mystica, quae est sapientia experimentalis et non doctrinalis. Quia nemo novit nisi qui accipit hoc negotium absconditum.
>
> (According to St. Augustine, God has to fulfill everything: but since natural emptiness is not possible, spiritual emptiness is even less so.—And for this reason you shall be silent: for the ultimate silence . . . And from this follows that this whole sermon evolves from mystical theology which draws its knowledge from experience and not from doctrine. Nobody comprehends this unless he accepts this hidden detachment.)[28]

This example should also demonstrate how key notions of Tauler's could be directly and accurately heard in later centuries, fermenting new ideas.

Tauler's Christmas sermon is also an illustration for the second point of Eckhart's programmatic statement: the return into the Godhead. Indeed, it is given the major part in the homily. Recent commentators of this Eckhartian notion have stressed how different his understanding is from the tradition of gradual approachment, namely purification-illumination-union. Matthew Fox even named his collection of Eckhartian sermons according to a key notion and neologism of the master: *Breakthrough.*[29] This concept does not easily lend itself to the catechetic function of the sermon as does the traditional schema of three (or more) stages leading to spiritual perfection and mystical union. For at the very center of Eckhart's understanding of experiencing God is the presupposition that ultimately any way can be the way, and every way is also a nonway, because man can break through by detaching himself and being com-

---

28. The marginal notes were probably written in 1516; cf. *Weimarer Ausgabe*, vol. 9, 96f.

29. Matthew Fox, *Breakthrough: Meister Eckhart's Creation Spirituality in New Translation;* with introduction and commentaries (Garden City, N.Y., 1980). Cf. also Haas, loc. cit.194ff.

pletely open to God. In his Christmas sermon Tauler attempts to communicate this intellectual radicalism by balancing it against two traditional ways of relating the birth of Christ to the essence of the Holy Trinity and the image of the virgin birth. These two points provide the rhetorical framework for the major idea of the sermon, which, in general terms, corresponds to Eckhart's second precept in his programmatic statement: to become embedded in God.

There is a sermon by Eckhart on the same theme in which he takes the occasion of the Christmas night liturgy to speak of the threefold birth and silence.[30] In other words, the main theme is that to which Tauler alludes in the conclusion of his first sermon. It would be inappropriate to press a comparison of the two sermons to the point of parallel exegesis, but the difference between the two preachers is eloquent. While both Eckhart and Tauler insert numerous concordant passages from Scripture, move along a very clear threefold structure, and use their mystical stratagem of concepts and subconcepts to depict spiritual perfection and union, there are noticeable differences at many points, which distinguish the intellectual master from the pastoral-mystic disciple. Whereas Tauler refers to Saint Augustine several times in well-distributed pacing, Eckhart draws from a wider circle of references, including Dionysius. Tauler skillfully blends mystical notions with popular images, popular proverbs, and even down-to-earth exhortations in order to admonish his audience to observe proper behavior. Eckhart dwells in a world of biblical references and theological abstractions. It is moving to watch how both mystics perceptibly gravitate toward the same main concept in the context of Christmas. For Eckhart and Tauler, spiritual perfection means becoming free of sensual imagery—a true counter-theme to the event of the incarnation of Christ. At a central point in their divisions, they both quote Matthew 19:29: "Whoever leaves father and mother and all possessions for my sake shall receive a hundredfold and eternal life." They then develop the thought of abandonment of one's own free will as a precondition to truly experiencing the birth of Christ within us. Eckhart assembles a bold series of biblical quotations toward the closing and climactic prayer: "May the God who was reborn today as a human being help us in

---

30. Fox edition, 293–301; the thematic verse is Ws 18:14, "Dum silentium tenerent . . ./When peaceful silence lay all over" (Introitus for the Sunday of Christmas Week).

this birth! May he eternally help us weak human beings so that we may be born in him in a divine way. Amen."[31] Tauler, in a more laconic but also more concrete manner, ends with: "May God help us prepare a dwelling-place for this noble birth, so that we may all attain spiritual motherhood. Amen." I think these two supplications aptly illustrate the common foundation and the different attitudes of the two mystics. While Eckhart moves toward abstraction by way of translating Christ's birth into some reflections on human perception, Tauler stays much closer to biblical images, to pastoral immediacy, and to maintaining, in a metonymic form, part of the biblical event in order to move his audience.

The rhetorical context of the Dominican sermon as preached by Tauler has two features that, in practical terms, are of importance: the liturgical connotation and the manner of reception and preservation. The sermons were given to (predominantly female) monastic audiences and addressed people whose education did not match that of the preacher in terms of scholastic training. The audience, however, was literate and educated in general terms. The sermon is thus not to be mistaken for the ordinary popular homily delivered to public parishes.[32] The preacher was usually available for Sundays and feast days, and he combined his homiletic office with other duties such as that of confessor. Only in exceptional circumstances did he form a personal and close bond to the communities as did Tauler— if we are to believe historical record, the duty was considered a burden and assigned to the younger priests.[33] But before the question is raised of how these sermons were recorded, collated, and handed down to a wider audience and later generations, a specific sermon will be used to exemplify how we can deduce the direct interaction between the preacher Tauler and his listeners.

A recent study analyzing the styles of Eckhart, Tauler, and Suso by means of computer-aided programming of syntactic patterns and idiosyncracies has led the author, Gabriele von Siegroth-

---

31. Fox edition, 301.
32. Herbert Grundmann, "Geschichtliche Grundlagen der deutschen Mystik," in Kurt Ruh, Hrsg., *Altdeutsche und Altniederländische Mystik* (Wege der Forschung XXIII; Darmstadt, 1964), 82ff.
33. Heribert Christian Scheeben, "Über die Predigtweise der deutschen Mystiker"; ibid., 101ff.

Nellessen, to an interesting set of conclusions.[34] She found Tauler the most spontaneous and audience-oriented preacher of the three. Since her syntactic method relies on the Middle High German and is accessible only to the specialist, I restrict myself to the rhetorical part of her argumentation, amplifying it from other sources and viewing it in a wider framework. She chooses the sermon on a text from the Epistle for the Fifth Sunday after Trinity (H 40); the sermon thematizes prayer, but it is also an example of how Tauler perceptibly distances himself from radical Eckhartian notions.[35] However, Tauler also deviates from the traditional understanding by offering at least three, if not more, of his own key notions. While Eckhart prefers to follow the pattern of the treatise even while preaching, Tauler relates to the everyday context of the audience. He presents points of reflection that are almost self-contained units without caring too much for a strict logical disposition. Sentences are comparatively short and reflect an oral pattern. In rhetorical terms, he follows one of the eight precepts of Humbert of Romans: the topic of religious experience (*scientia experimentalis*).[36] This requires that the preacher know the appropriate language (*aptum*) and have insight into the disposition of the target audience (*status animarum*). He can thus rely on a host of enthymemes (presuppositions that are either impossible or unnecessary to prove because they are commonly shared by the preacher and his listeners).

Tauler opens the sermon with a thematic three-point division: nature, essence and method, locality (third of twenty-eight paragraphs in the American translation). This partition is introduced in the form of a direct address to his audience. He then seems to make a traditional scholastic distinction regarding the essence of prayer. Here, "traditional" means according to John of Damascene, Saint Anselm, and Saint Augustine: Prayer is the ascent of mind and heart to God (*ascensus mentis in Deum*). But Tauler dispenses of it in one sentence and immediately turns to the other main points of his division. In fact, it soon becomes obvious that he is developing only

---

34. *Versuch einer exakten Stilbeschreibung für Meister Eckhart, Johannes Tauler und Heinrich Seuse* (Medium Aevum 38; München, 1979). The analysis of the sermon discussed is to be found on pp. 221–251.

35. See Alois M. Haas, "Wege und Grenzen mystischer Erfahrung"; in *Sermo Mysticus, Studien zu Theologie und Sprache der deutschen Mystik* (Dokimion 4; Freiburg, 1979), 147ff.

36. Haas, ibid., 147.

the third point, and this in a most unusual fashion: when and where to pray. The fifth paragraph opens with another direct address to the audience ("Now I would like to talk briefly about the nature and method of prayer") but steers right off in the direction of the old mystical schema of three stages of perfection as evidenced in proficiency in praying: neophytes, practitioners, and those who have attained excellence (*incipientes, proficientes, perfecti*). This is soon followed by another mystical tradition, firmly established since Dionysius: the external and the inner eye. From this example, it follows that Tauler was not observing the rules that apply to a harmonious rhetorical argumentation according to his stated partition; instead, he anchors these underlying concepts without specific transitions in the practical life of ordinary vices and vanities ("all kinds of frivolities"). In the next direct address (seventh paragraph; "Beloved . . ."), he ventures into a totally new idea and a favorite theme of his: detachment in order to be totally immersed in God. The following paragraph (again in the form of reiterating direct appeals) is a harsh condemnation of institutional forms of devotion if they are hindering spiritual progress, and a whole series of prayers are mentioned by name. It offers a beautiful example of how Tauler prefers the ad hoc image to any kind of logical rigor ("This prayer in spirit . . ."). At first sight, the analogy of sacred communal effort and stages and contexts of spiritual prayer seems to flow naturally. However, when one ponders where the combining element of the analogy actually lies, and what the traditional simile-formula "And so it is with spiritual prayer . . ." transcendingly translates, one realizes that Tauler has not outlined this in any clear or concise fashion. One may contemplate such an analogy, but it is certainly not spelled out. When he reaches the meditation on the Holy Trinity (paragraph 11, "The Heavenly Father . . .") he has moved away from the Epistle, his partition, and the previous points—only an audience accustomed to such a texture of mystical meditation could follow the train of thought of this preacher.[37] For Christian unanimity in praying as set out in the theme of the biblical passage has become almost totally reoriented to mystical "single-mindedness in prayer" (penultimate paragraph).

One objection to such an analysis might be that many jumps

---

37. Siegroth-Nelleson, at the end of her analysis of this sermon, sees the "inconsequential" structure of Tauler in slightly negative terms.

and turns of a loose structure could be interpreted as effects of oral tradition and that since preservation and collation of manuscripts literally involved many hands, "corrupt" texts are to be expected. Many obscure and distorted passages are due to such causes in the history of reception. But one has to remind oneself that these sermons were given by a mendicant preacher who was trained to prepare carefully. He surely exercised control over most transcriptions done by one or more listeners. We can safely assume that usually the preacher provided the general disposition in written form, that nuns or other religious persons composed a transcription, and that the preacher then approved the medieval equivalent of a modern final version. The role of later scribes and copyists has, of course, to be remembered when analyzing the finer points of language with arguments concerning devotional texts of that time.

Another distinctive feature of Tauler's preserved work is that it is written exclusively in Middle High German. This has to be kept in mind when entering a discussion of how medieval mysticism raised the vernacular to the level of the substance and flexibility of Latin in the course of a few decades. Subtlety of argumentation, as in the case of Meister Eckhart, often surpassed that of Latin works by the very same person. Furthermore, there was a dynamic force inherent in the training of a preacher who was steeped in Latin scholastic tradition, but was also thoroughly familiar with popular culture in the vernacular—and who expressed himself to an audience that had no direct access to the Latin tradition.

Tauler's sermons do not show signs of systematic or direct use of popular ancillary manuals (in manuscript form) such as Caesarius of Heisterbach's *Dialogus miraculorum* (ca. 1222), a collection of miraculous anecdotes; the *Gesta romanorum* (around 1300); or the *Physiologus*, the most popular collection of animal-allegories dating back to antiquity. The reason is fairly evident: Tauler was interested in conveying a mystic message, and his sermons are not directed at the broad masses even though they are public in character.[38] Another form of model was, of course, collections of sermons of famous preachers of that time, usually arranged according to moral categories (vices and virtues), occasions (on death, etc.), and, less often, according to the liturgical year.

---

38. Alan of Lille, 19, points out that one of the most telling signs of hereticism is the sermon preached in secrecy.

INTRODUCTION

Tauler's distinctive orientation toward mystical spirituality in preaching shines through when one compares his texts with those of great spiritual masters who must have been part of his theological education. He learned from them, as was remarked above, in the form of medieval textbooks that contained excerpts or "sentences" organized according to various themes. I shall conclude this section on preaching by comparing two of his sermons, selected at random, with equivalent texts of theologians of the first order who were great preachers and mystics, Saint Augustine and Saint Bernard of Clairvaux (1091–1153).

Saint Augustine's thirty-fourth treatise of his *Admonitio de sequentibus in Ioannem tractatibus* deals with John 8:12,[39] "*Ego sum lux mundi*/I am the light of the world," the textual basis of Tauler's Sermon on the Fifth Sunday in Lent (H 10). As is to be expected, the Church Father and master rhetorician presents in his treatise a point-by-point development of distinctions of the concert of light. Although Tauler quotes Augustine toward the end of his sermon, a comparison yields just this reference but hardly any other points of the conceptual framework of the treatise.[40] Analogies or parallels are coincidental and not set in any parallel system of points of reference. In the case of Saint Bernard's *Sermo in Ascensione Domini*, the same thema (Mk 16:14: "When the eleven disciples were sitting together") serves as a point of departure.[41] But the directions taken already begin to differ in the prothema. Saint Bernard states it as an extension of "*benignitas et humanitas Salvatoris*." He then expands on the notion that we can learn goodness by aiding faith with good works. Numerous biblical references structure the short and concise exhortation. Tauler, on the contrary, after having briefly dealt with the thema of hardheartedness, quickly develops two mystical prothemes: living water and true love. He builds the former into an illustrative and extended allegory of the cistern (containing only

---

39. Migne, *Patrologiae Latinae*, tom. XXXV, 1652–1657.
40. The quotation as given by Tauler: "The great sun has created for itself a lesser sun, and veiled it in a cloud, not to render it invisible, but to temper its brightness so that we should be able to glance at it." Distinction 4 (1653/4) of St. Augustine goes as follows: "(Deum de Deo, lumen de lumine.) Per hoc lumen factum est solis lumen: et lumen quod fecit solem, sub quo fecit et nos, factum est sub sole propter nos. Factum est, inquam, propter nos sub sole lumen quod fecit solem. Noli contemnere nubem carnis: nube tegitur, non ut obscuretur, sed ut temperetur."
41. Migne, *Patrologiae Latinae*, CLXXXIII, 299–301.

putrid water) and reiterates the second notion of true love. After two concluding metaphors—the ship in the storm and the wounded knight—all is condensed into the supplication "let waters of pure love be poured into us," a rather remarkable move away from the homiletic entrance on Mark 16:14.

Tauler does occupy a very specific place in the history of medieval preaching mainly on account of his mystic spirituality. His sermons are part of a rich and dynamic tradition that flowed in a broad stream. It is impossible to locate precisely all the feeding sources, rivers, and inlets from which they emerged. But clearly he embodied in his work a spiritual quality that was eagerly perceived by his contemporaries and Christians of all denominations in the centuries to come.

MYSTICAL LANGUAGE

Saying the ineffable entails a dilemma inherent in all mystical expression. The ultimate impossibility of appropriate verbal expression is an intrinsic quality of the mystical relation between creature and Creator. The Christian tradition on this topic is rich and varied. Dionysios, an early exponent of the *via negativa*, noted at the end of his treatise:

> . . . he has no name; we cannot know him. . . . When we attribute something to him, or deny any or all of the things which he is not, we do not describe him or abolish him, nor in any way that we can understand do we affirm him or deny him. For the perfect and unique cause of all is of necessity beyond comparison with the highest of all imaginable heights, whether by affirmation or denial.[42]

Tauler echoes this perception when he expands on the theme in his Sermon II on the Feast of Blessed Trinity (H 29). He describes the Holy Trinity with such a powerful paradox as "imageless Image" or transposes a colloquialism to mystical depths: "When we come to

---

42. Cf. *The Cloud of Unknowing and Other Works*, trans. and introduced by Clifton Wolters (Harmondsworth, 1978), 217/18.

speak of the Most Blessed Trinity, we are at a loss for words." This sermon thematizes the superiority of experience over articulation, parallels silence with self-denial, and transforms this problem into a description of the mystical process itself.

Our contention that any form of mysticism happens in a very specific cultural context makes it necessary to dwell on Tauler's language in the form of a few short observations on the medieval German vernacular in its relation to mystical language of that time—this in order to show both the limitations and the possibilities of Middle High German and its partial formation by the mystical authors who employed it. They expanded the horizons of the vernacular as a social code in theological and psychological dimensions that even today inspire awe in the modern reader. Their heritage is still a living force in German intellectual discourse, whether in theology or in philosophy. In the nineteenth century, philosophers tried to do justice to this achievement by ascribing it to the idiosyncrasy of individual genius, especially that of Eckhart. But modern research has convincingly demonstrated that the collective achievement of German mystics was not so much the creation and invention of myriads of neologisms; rather they were able, in the span of a few decades, to raise the vernacular to the level—and often beyond—of the scholarly Latin of their day.[43] The limitations stem from a fact directly accessible to the American reader, whose language contains many Germanic words whose meanings remain in part identical with the German ones (cognate). Middle High German, like the English language of that day, however, possessed some properties absent from the modern language, and had a range of connotations not spontaneously accessible to the reader of our day. Let us, therefore, exemplify these general conditions in concrete semantic terms. This will then be used to trace one of Tauler's most beautiful passages in a particular train of thought of that generally considered his central mystical conception and intellectual creation: the ground of the soul.

Middle High German, like the English language of that period, was fluid and in a state of transition. The mystic was an essential

---

43. Alois M. Haas, "Meister Eckhart und die Sprache, Sprachgeschichtliche und sprachtheologische Aspekte seines Werks," in *Geistliches Mittelalter* (Dokimion 8; Freiburg 1984), 199ff. A systematic view of the problem is given in B. Q. Morgan and F. W. Strothman, eds., *Middle High German Translation of the Summa Theologica by Thomas Aquinas* (New York, 1967; 1st ed. 1950).

part of the dynamics of the process in that he or she had specific linguistic requirements that came directly from their predicament, for example, their need for apophatic language. To say the ineffable in appropriate terms entailed the prolific use of negative morphemes with verbs, nouns, and adjectives. Some are still alive (*entziehen* = to withdraw), others are virtually untranslatable even into modern German (*entwerden* = *zu Nichts werden* = to become nothing). There are morphemes that can no longer be used in compositions but that were possible in the older language. When Tauler bursts into a description of the divine dimension of the soul and has her become "*got-var, gotlich, gottig*" (V 37;146,21) only the second epithet can be rendered into high German without loss (*güottlich* = godly, divine)—the first and the third do not exist any more (they would be: *gottbar, gottig*), and hence the problem arises as to how to translate this threefold differentiation of "divine."[44] In the case of abstract nouns (*Gottheit* = Godhead) the distinction often lies in a partially changed meaning of a lexem (*arbeit* = work; but in Middle High German it also means the travails of a knight on his quest). The considerable linguistic distance from Middle High German, therefore, causes serious difficulties even at the level of intertranslatability within its own language tradition.[45] The condition becomes more complex, of course, when translation into another language—even into one that is a linguistic relative—takes place.

The word *grunt* is of Germanic origin and had many connotations, some of which are still present in their modern from (*der Grund* = ground, reason, etc.). Etymologically, the first meaning (lower part of a physical entity, topographical or human) is still visible in the modern notion of "buildings and grounds." This notion became configurative by acquiring the intellectual meaning of "fundamental, basic." Tauler successfully combined literal and figurative meaning in a mystical context by describing the innermost dwelling-place of mystical union with this word, and by signifying that this is also a dynamic process, he transferred yet another connotation into the concept. But before its actual usage is demonstrated, some medieval

---

44. This passage is not contained in E. Colledge's and Sister M. Jane's partial translation of this particular sermon; but their excerpt does include a highly instructive statement by Tauler, reflecting on his use of the vernacular: "Not everyone will understand what I am saying, though I always speak plain German" (p. 77).

45. The problem is briefly discussed (with references) by Alois M. Haas in his introduction to HXIV.

connotations have to be reviewed. The word was not simply an equivalent of one particular Latin term like *fundus* or a string of terms.[46] It did, however, have a pre-coined elective affinity in that the description of chivalresque love poetry put the center of tender feelings at the *herzens grunt* (= bottom of the heart). Another important derivation is word formations that, in part, are common to German and English: *grundelôs* (groundless), *gruntlich* (thorough), *gründen* (to base something upon something, etc.)—their modern usage still reflects some of the literal and figurative meanings confluent in the root word *grunt*. The matter becomes more complex when Tauler, by way of standard German (and English) word transformation—the addition of a preposition—changes the basic lexem into a composite when using the biblical image of "abyss" (unfortunately, at this stage the cognate character to the English semantic equivalent is lost): *abgrunt*. But the semantic incorporation of the most fundamental meaning of "ground" into one of the principal lexical markers for infinity and the relationship between man and God has reached a density, and at the same time diversity, of connotation such that all these underlying significations become accessible only to the contemplative mind versed in this kind of reflection.[47]

Sermon 24 on 1 Peter 4:8 ("Live wisely, and keep your senses awake to greet the hours of prayer") is an example of how Tauler adapts the biblical notion to his terminology, and of how he, by means of traceable amplification, enriches the ground of the soul, which then becomes the concluding expression of union and divinization. Tauler's theme is the division of prayer (= spirit of discernment; given in the second of sixteen paragraphs) into "detachment, abandonment, inwardness, and single-mindedness." The sermon is unusually rich in the development of concrete images from everyday life, in particular the change of seasons for the farmer and the tilling of the "ground." Tauler even includes the observation that the preparation for a feast day is the time when "the kitchen abounds in sweet fragrances of rich and rare dishes" (fifth paragraph). A prothema,

---

46. For this possibility, cf. the excellent article by Paul Wyser, o.p., "Taulers Terminologie vom Seelengrund," in Kurt Ruh, 324–352, where he carefully delineates this and other possible Latin roots, 328ff. He revises some earlier observations of Hermann Kunisch, *Das Wort 'Grund' in der Sprache der deutschen Mystik* (Münster, 1929).

47. Cf. Josef Quint, "Mystik und Sprache: Ihr Verhältnis zueinander, insbesondere in der spekulativen Mystik Meister Eckharts," in Kurt Ruh, 113–151, where a rich selection of material (in a German context) is presented by an authority in the field.

restated in paragraph twelve ("*Fratres, sobrii estote et vigilate*" is a very familiar Psalm verse from the prayer of the hours), is translated as "For true prayer is a direct raising of the mind and heart to God, without intermediary (MHG *unmittelichen*). This and nothing else is the essence of prayer."

I would now like to list the distinctions of this particular amplification of prayer (traditionally it is the seventh, expounding the property of things) and point out where and how Tauler switches his mystical code from "prayer" to "achieving the state of discernment" in the mystical union of, and in, the "innermost ground." Toward the end of paragraph thirteen, Tauler specifies that through "essential," "true," and eventually "heavenly" prayer, God may enter the soul's "deepest ground" (MHG *innerlichsten grunt*) where alone there is "undifferentiated unity." In the next paragraph, he introduces (following Saint Augustine) the etymological/biblical amplification that the core of the soul really is a "hidden abyss" (MHG *verborgen appetgrunde*) which is also an "abyss of love" ("Into this noble and wondrous ground" = MHG "*In dem edlen minneclichen abgrunde*"). In the next (penultimate or fifteenth) paragraph, the abyss changes its connotation in that it is God whom all truly praying men embrace in "this same abyss" (MHG *daz selbe abgrunde*). They "gaze back to this loving abyss" (MHG *der minnen abgrunde*), "until they return to the loving, dark, silent rest of the abyss" (MHG *in das minnenkliche dunster stille rasten in dem abgrunde*). The conclusion: "Thus they go in and out, and yet remain at all times within, in the sweet silent ground (MHG *minneclichen stillen abgrunde*) in which they have their substance and life." A description of the divinization that arises from such a contemplative state follows. The enumeration of identical attributes for "prayer" and "ground" are meant to initiate the listener into the notion of elective affinity between man and God. The transformation of a state of praying into a state of actual being is expressed as mystical oration; for the etymological derivation of "ground" as the core of man becoming totally immersed in the "derivation" (*Abgrund* = God) verbally parallels the course of spiritual transformation. This, then, would be one of the more sublime examples of how Tauler the mystic preacher develops the conceptual understanding of the "imageless Image," saying the ineffable.

INTRODUCTION

THE MYSTIC WAY

So far, the mystic pattern has been shown to be interwoven within the threads of the the social and intellectual life of the fourteenth century. Let us now consider the actuality of Tauler's mystical message, and try to decipher the specificity of his way as articulated in our collection of sermons and as lived out by the Dominican nuns, the Friends of God, and others. Besides the devotees of Eckhart, Tauler, and Suso, a variety of other movements, groups, and communities exerted a far-reaching influence and appeal:

> . . . the relationship between the sanctity of the fourteenth century and the normal Christian piety was complex . . . mystical experiences were dramatic manifestations of a devotional trend which, translated into the vernacular idiom and transformed for a secular milieu by writers such as Eckhart, was increasingly popular in the later Middle Ages.[48]

There was, for example, the Franciscan tradition, beautifully enshrined in one of its basic texts, *The Soul's Journey into God* by Saint Bonaventure (1217–1274), which is in the form of a lucid and poetic treatise.[49] The Modern Devotion also emerged at this time. Its founder, Gert Groote (1340–1384), was actually a lay preacher. In his youth, he was deeply influenced by the German and Dutch mystics, particularly Meister Eckhart and John Ruusbroec.[50] There were many other spiritual movements that were essentially mystical. In the case of Tauler, the foremost question is less what kind of movement he joined, or represented, than his relation to his spiritual mentor, Meister Eckhart.

This question can be better answered when one keeps in mind the broader spiritual context of the age. Steven Ozment has summarized the three central features of medieval Christian mysticism,

---

48. Richar Kieckhefer, *Unquiet Souls: Fourteenth Century Saints and Their Religious Milieu* (Chicago and London, 1984), 165.

49. In Ewert Cousins, trans. and ed., *Bonaventure* (Classics of Western Spirituality; New York, Ramsey, Toronto, 1978), 51–116.

50. R. R. Post, *The Modern Devotion: Confrontation with Reformation Humanism* (Leiden, 1968). The author points out, however, that apart from exceptions (like Gerlach Peters, 338f.), the movement itself quickly turned against mysticism, cf. especially chapter 8.

of which Tauler is both an heir and an integral factor, as follows.[51]
A first feature was the dichotomy of traditions. The Latin tradition
drew heavily on a traditional monastic spirituality, which was rooted
firmly in the writings of Dionysius the Areopagite, prejudiced toward will, and emphasized practical piety, while remaining Chris-
tocentric in nature. Another tradition, emerging from the
Dominican Order, tended to be more intellectual, striving for a
merger with the divine abyss rather than the imitation of Christ and
conformity with Him, while remaining decidedly Neoplatonist in
theology. A second feature was the belief common to nearly all medieval mystics that "the religious realities in faith can actually be experienced." The Germanic mystical tradition furnished the two
most widely popular elements in this notion of the intrinsically divine nature of man: Eckhart's spark of the soul (*scintilla animae* or *syn-
teresis*) and Tauler's ground of the soul (*Seelengrund*) encompass a
vision of the soul returning into God by returning into itself. A third
notion of the German mystics is closely related to this essential condition: Withdrawal from the world enables man to become "like
God" again by transcending the physical limitations of human existence. These three features are not necessarily separable entities;
however, they will be used to follow Tauler's mystic way.

From our introduction we know that Tauler's general position
in the broad tradition tended toward an intellectual conciliation of
the more abstract German mysticism with the Latin tradition.[52]

1. With regard to the Neoplatonic heritage, Tauler saw himself
as a disciple of Eckhart, a master to whom he refers several times in
his sermons in a loving and respectful way. In the Sermon on the
Eve before Palm Sunday, for example, he concludes a description of
divine union with this remark:

> That was the teaching and these were the words of a most lovable
> master, but you did not comprehend. For he spoke about eter-
> nity, and you understood it in temporal terms. Beloved, if I have
> said too much, forgive me, I shall gladly restrain myself; but for
> God there can never be too much.[53]

---

51. Steven E. Ozment, *The Age of Reform*, 115–117.
52. Steven E. Ozment implied this in *Homo Spiritualis: A Comparative Study of the
Anthropology of Johannes Tauler, Jean Gerson and Martin Luther (1509–16) in the Context of Their
Theological Thought* (Leiden, 1969), 13–26.
53. H 15b, 103.

This passage should also remind one of an important condition of Tauler's absorption of Eckhartian mysticism: Eckhart's trial for heresy had ended in a posthumous condemnation of some of the master's more controversial and enigmatic (Latin and German) statements.[54] The disciple must have been conscious that too bold a formulation might lead to something similar. But Tauler maintains like Eckhart that man, before emanating from God, was "one essential being" with, and in, God. A central aim of his mystic thrust is, therefore, the articulation of the desire to reenter into this precreated purity. It is not surprising, then, that Tauler utilizes a host of well-known Neoplatonic imagery when preaching homilies on the Gospel of Saint John (III, H 10; XIV, H 44; XVI, H 59). However, Tauler's inclusion of more traditional mystical precepts was less out of cautious deference than from his role as a spiritual director (*lebmeister*); pastoral practice was directed toward very specific individuals and communities. This must explain his seemingly effortless transition from moral admonition to mystical exhortation, as demonstrated in the following conclusion of the Sermon on the Sunday after Ascension:

> All I have preached to you in this sermon is addressed to the spiritual man; let him bear the counsels continually in mind, and let him regulate his conduct accordingly. It will be quite possible for him to do so when the tranquillity of his soul is rooted and grounded in God; when his desire is directed wholly toward God. In this light he will know and understand all virtues for what they are, sloughing them off by the help of Christ. This is the way of all those who are born anew and are strengthened interiorly in true detachment. The more this interior process increases, the more richly the Holy Spirit is given, the more gloriously received. (H 23)

The ascent from virtuous conduct of life to illuminated detachment in God is clearly visible. In this Tauler differs from Eckhart. A good example is their differing attitudes toward the main object of pious devotion of the time, the veneration of the Passion (which often led to quite ostentatious behavior). In the last sermon of our collection,

---

54. Cf. E. Colledge's presentation of the trial and the resulting circumstances in *Meister Eckhart*, 11ff.

the commemoration of the Exaltation of the Cross, Tauler gradually interiorizes the gesture of ascent into a description of the soul in what to him is the highest ascent: the return of the created spirit into God. Eckhart, in a comparable homily, does not differ from Tauler, but he moves directly into the significance of the event, without including the more traditional stepping up of levels of meaning.[55] Tauler's sermons abound in practical spiritual advice: how to avoid mechanical prayer, habitual sins (X, H 33), exalted enthusiasms (II, H 2), and the positive benefits of sacramental life (III, H 10). In fact, in one sermon (XV, H 55), the expected mystical theme of divinization (Feast of Our Lady's Nativity) is quickly redirected into down-to-earth advice on detachment from earthly possessions.

Tauler often has harsh words for higher learning not directly linked with spirituality. Such utterances have to be read in context, and not construed as an overt or covert criticism of the Church Fathers from whom Tauler derived his spiritual knowledge. A rather moving example of this attitude is the second interpretation of the Feast of the Blessed Trinity (H 29). Note how Tauler affirms the authority of Saint Thomas in relation to the problem at hand, a description of the Holy Trinity:

> Scholars discuss this image a great deal, trying to express in various ways its nature and essence. They all assert that it belongs to the highest faculties of our soul, which are memory, intellect, and will; that these faculties enable us to receive and enjoy the Blessed Trinity. This is indeed true, but it is the lowest degree of perception, leaving the mystery in the natural order. Saint Thomas says that the perfection of the image lies in its activity, in the exercise of the faculties; that is, in the active memory, in the active intellect, and the active will. Further than that, Saint Thomas will not go.

A bit further on in the sermon, Tauler cites Christ's statement "The kingdom of God is within us," and he comments: "It is to be found in the inmost depth, beyond the activities of our faculties." This shows how Tauler very consciously distinguished between the doctrine and the mystical way. The homilist prefaces the above refer-

---

55. Bernard McGinn, *Meister Eckhart*, 46.

ence to Saint Thomas with a reflection on a central image of Neoplatonic tradition: rebirth.

> You, however, should allow the Holy Trinity to be born in the center of your soul, not by the use of human reason, but in essence and truth; not in words but in reality. It is the divine mystery we seek, and how we are truly its image; for this divine image certainly dwells in our souls by nature, actually, truly, and distinctly, though of course not in as lofty a manner as it is in Itself.

However, it is not so much the traditional aspect I would like to emphasize as the opposition of word/reality. For Tauler, if we read him correctly, did not experience that ultimate union which so many of his contemporaries professed to have achieved. Why, then, the incessant homiletic attempt to transmit what the spiritual counsellor himself has not seen: union with and in God? It is here that Tauler moves beyond Eckhart along his own path. He justifies and explains his spiritual activities by anchoring them in concrete pastoral concerns and catechetic advice.[56] By clearly designating the ultimate state of being into an eschatological time and an infinite space, Tauler develops the concept of faith as nonexperience, as the recognition and acceptance of human limitation. In many of his sermons he refers to a traditional stage of mystical experience: the night of desolation, isolation, and utter desertedness. He then goes on to assert that because he and others do not come into this experience during earthly life, their faith carries the Church. Nonexperience is thus thematized as mystic faith expressed in faithful preaching.

2. Steven Ozment's second assertion concerns the creation and formulation of basic conceptions of German mysticism that became distinguishable elements of the medieval tradition. In the case of Tauler, judging from the influence of his legacy, two conceptual formulations have drawn particular attention: the formula *grunt und gemuete* and his understanding of the abandonment of one's will and submission to God's: detachment or *Gelassenheit*.[57]

Meister Eckhart left a treatise, *On Detachment*, which charts in

---

56. Alois M. Haas, "Sprache und mystische Erfahrung nach Tauler und Seuse," in *Geistliches Mittelalter*, 240–242. He draws his examples mainly from V 40 and 41.

57. Cf. Alois Haas, "Johannes Tauler," in *Sermo mysticus*, 255–295, where he incorporated findings in condensed form from an earlier study, *Nim dîn selbes war: Studien zur Selbsterkenntnihei Meister Eckhart, Johann Tauler und Heinrich Seuse* (Freiburg, 1971).

a short and concise form the function of the virtue of detachment for the mystical way.[58] By freeing himself from earthly things, man prepares the soul to receive God, to become uniform with God, and to become "susceptible" to divine inflowing. The spiritual context is that of ultimate humility. Tauler uses the concept of detachment in many forms: as a preparatory stage that varies in different people (VI, H 23), or as the decisive, all-embracing act enabling one to become immersed in the ground of the soul, the divine abyss (VII, 24). The two sermons of the present collection provide an excellent sense of how Tauler understands and uses the concept. As in Eckhart, the soul readies itself for divinization by achieving true detachment. However, Tauler instills a strong sense of self-denial and abandonment of self-will, a volitional dimension into the terms describing this disposition that had not been there before. This remains noticeable in the mystical tradition, especially in the highly influential *Theologia Germanica*, a tract written about ten years after Tauler's death by the anonymous Franckforter around 1370.[59] Again, it is almost impossible to render directly into English the semantic associogramms the medieval author used. Detachment entails, for instance, the notion of active passivity, a condition poignantly mirrored in the verb *leiden* where various meanings (to suffer, to like, to pass through, etc.) are matched by the functional duality of expressing something both transitively and intransitively and becoming an almost matching expression of "striving for perfect self-surrender."[60]

The *gemuete* and the "ground" of the soul have received extensive and penetrating treatment by Ozment.[61] After the short linguistic commentary on the word *Grund* in the preceding section of this introduction, we might quote Ozment's conceptual summary in which he identifies the two terms as anthropological motifs belonging to the Neoplatonic and Augustinian traditions. From a multiple usage characteristic of Tauler, the "ground of the soul" emerges as a "naturally given and firmly established dwelling-place in the soul where God is present and from which he neither can, nor desires to, separate Himself." The *gemuete* (the High German *Geist* is a pale

---

58. E. Colledge and B. McGinn, *Meister Eckhart*, 285–297. Cf. also McGinn's commentary on p. 47.
59. Bengt Hoffmann, ed., *The Theologia Germanica of Martin Luther*; preface by Bengt Häglund (Classics of Western Spirituality; New York, Ramsey, Toronto, 1980).
60. Kieckhefer, 71.
61. Ozment, *Homo Spiritualis*, 22.

translation) resembles most closely the Latin *mens* (mind) and is "an active power, grounded in and emerging from this 'ground,' which embraces the powers of the soul (i.e., reason and will) and directs and draws the creature back to his origin in uncreatedness by first drawing him into the created and subsequently into the uncreated ground of the soul." The two terms very closely resemble Eckhart's "spark of the soul"; the conclusion of Sermon 5 (H 19; Ascension II) uses the central image of the master in this very context.

3. Of all the notions used by medieval German mystics, *vergottung* (divinization) caused the greatest misunderstanding and error—on the part of the medieval inquisitor, or, for that matter, the nineteenth-century romantic or philosopher.[62] What Ozment described above as a medieval mystic's insistence on "becoming 'like God' " is indeed a complex theological area describing innumerable aspects of the relationship between Creator and creation. Another cause for confusion lies in the fact that mystical union as the ultimate aim of any spiritual activity was "conventionally" seen in the spousal imagery of the Song of Songs. Tauler naturally knew this (cf. IV, H18); he not only refers to the biblical book but also its treatment by one of the great medieval commentators, Richard of Saint Victor. John Ruusbroec, a contemporary and student of Tauler's sermons, also made bridal imagery the central point of reference for his presentation of the mystic way. Tauler's decision to use other imagery in order to arrive at an apt description of seeing the ineffable, the imageless Image, the unfathomable abyss, therefore, warrants a final hypothesis.

Hans Urs von Balthasar, in describing Tauler's distinctive mystical way, points out how Tauler uses, almost in conflict with Eckhart's perception, the images of the noble and Godlike soul to set forth the image of man's will to empty itself for the Godhead.[63] Haas, too, stresses Tauler's firm and unwavering tendency toward a spirituality of the Passion of Christ and the Holy Trinity.[64] We may assume that the imagery from the Song of Songs merits only occasional mention since it is not part of the union as Tauler de-

---

62. A highly instructive study of why and how the modern age could read its own theorems into the work of medieval mystics—a question of reading truly out of context—is given in Wolfram Malte Fues, *Mystik als Erkenntnis; Kritische Studien zur Meister Eckhart Forschung* (Studien zur Germanistik, Anglistik und Komparatistik, Bd. 102; Bonn 1981).

63. Loc. cit., 413.

64. Haas, "Johannes Tauler," 289–295.

scribes it in the traditional pattern of saying the ineffable, the paradox. As the imageless Image, the prayer transformed into divine silence, the search, having found ultimate tranquillity in the unfathomable abyss of the ground of the soul—Tauler's mystic way was one of genuine prostration. He was preaching in the context of an everyday medieval reality that he tried to make translucent for men of good will, enabling them to return to what he perceived to be the ultimate union: the return into God.

SERMON 1
[CHRISTMAS]

Puer natus est nobis et filius datus est nobis
A child is born to us, a son is given to us (Is 9:5)

This Sermon on the threefold birth, which Tauler preached on Christmas Day, is taken from the three Holy Masses of this solemn feast. It instructs us to collect the three faculties of the soul, and renounce our will, our desire, and our worldly activity within it.

Today Holy Christendom commemorates a threefold birth, which should so gladden and delight the heart that, enraptured with joyful love and jubilation, we should soar upward with sheer gratitude and bliss. And whoever cannot experience this ought to be quite distressed.

The first birth, and the most sublime, is that in which the Heavenly Father begets His only Son within the divine Essence, yet distinct in Person. The second birth we commemorate is that of maternal fruitfulness brought about in virginal chastity and true purity. The third birth is effected when God is born within a just soul every day and every hour truly and spiritually, by grace and out of love. These are the three births observed in today's three Holy Masses.

The first, we celebrate in the darkness of night, and it begins with the words: "The Lord has said to me: you are my Son, this day have I begotten You." This Mass points to the hidden birth which happens within the secrecy of the unknown Godhead. The second Mass starts with the words: "This day shall a light shine upon us." And here is meant the radiance of human nature divinized. This Mass begins in the darkness of night, and ends in the brightness of day, for it was partly known and partly unknown.

The third Mass is solemnized in the brightness of noon, and it commences thus: "A child is born to us, a Son is given to us." It signifies that very sweet birth which should and does occur every day and every moment within every just and holy soul if only it directs its attention lovingly toward that goal. For if it is to experience such a birth, it must turn inward and reverse all its faculties. Then God will give Himself in such a high measure, and surrender Himself so utterly that this gift will exceed anything the soul may ever have possessed.

We read in Holy Scripture that a child is born to us, and a Son is given to us, which is to say that He is ours, He belongs to us in a special way, above all ways; that He is begotten in us always, without ceasing. It is of this very sweet birth, referred to in the last of the three Masses, that we wish to speak first.

In order to attain to this wondrous birth, so that it may bear noble and rich fruit, we should consider the first—the paternal—birth, by which the Father begets His Son in eternity; for the superabundance of the Father's divine goodness is such that it transcends all human ways. It keeps back nothing, and this causes an eternal outpouring and communicating. For this reason Boethius and Saint Augustine say that it is God's nature and character to pour Himself out and to communicate; and thus the Father pours Himself forth in the Processions of the divine Persons and then on into creatures. Saint Augustine says further: "Because God is good, we are; and any good that creatures possess derives alone from the essential goodness of God."

What, then, should we observe about the paternal generation, and how should we perceive it? Note that the Father, distinct as Father, turns inward to Himself with His divine Intellect and penetrates in clear self-beholding the essential abyss of His eternal Being. In this act of pure self-comprehension He utters Himself completely by a Word; and the Word is His Son. And the act whereby He knows Himself is the generation of the Son in eternity. Thus He rests within Himself in the unity of essence, and He flows out in the distinction of Persons.

And so He turns inward, comprehending Himself, and He flows outward in the generation of His Image (that of His Son), which He has known and comprehended. And again He returns to Himself in perfect self-delight. And this delight streams forth as ineffable love, and that ineffable love is the Holy Spirit. Thus God turns inward, goes outward, and returns to Himself again. And these Processions happen for the sake of their return. Hence the celestial orbit is the noblest and most perfect, for it constantly returns to the origin and source from which it emerged. And for the same reason the human circuit, in its essential meaning, is the noblest and most perfect when it returns again to its source.

Now the specific character which the Heavenly Father possesses in this divine circulation should also be adopted by us if we are to attain spiritual motherhood in our soul. We, too, must completely turn inward in order to go out again. How, then, can this be accomplished?

The soul has three faculties, and in these it is the true image of the Blessed Trinity—memory, understanding, and free will. With their aid the soul is able to grasp God and to partake of Him, so that it becomes capable of receiving all that God is and can bestow. They enable the soul to contemplate eternity, for the soul is created between time and eternity. With its highest part it touches eternity, whereas with its lower part—that of the sensible and animal powers—it is bound up with time. Now because of the way these two powers are intertwined (due to the fall), the soul has turned toward time and temporal things. Accordingly, transitory things come easily to the soul, and it tends to love itself in them, thus turning to time and away from eternity.

We can see now that a reversal must necessarily take place if such a birth is to occur. There must be a definite introversion, a gathering up, an inward recollection of faculties without any dispersal, for in unity lies strength. So a marksman who wishes to hit his target more accurately shuts one eye to focus with greater precision. Whoever wishes to comprehend something clearly applies all his senses and concentrates them in the soul from which they have arisen. For just as all the branches of a tree spring from one trunk, so also must all powers of the soul be gathered up within its ground. And this is the introversion we are speaking of.

Moreover, should a going forth, an elevation beyond and above ourselves ever come about, then we must renounce our own will, desire, and worldly activity, so that we can orient ourselves single-mindedly toward God, and meet Him only in complete abandonment of self. What should remain is a pure cleaving to God alone, a making room for Him, Who is the highest and the nearest, so that His work can prosper, and His birth can be accomplished without hindrance. For if two are to become one, one must be passive whereas the other must act. If, for instance, my eye is to receive an image on the wall, or anything whatever, it must first be free from other images; for if there remained an image of color, it could not receive another. The same is true of the ear: If it already perceived a sound, it cannot hear another. In short, whatever should receive must first be empty, passive, and free.

In regard to this Saint Augustine said: "Pour out that you may be filled, go out of yourself, so that you may enter." And in another passage he comments: "Noble soul, sublime creature, why are you seeking Him outside yourself when He dwells wholly, truly, and purely within you? Why do you, a partaker of divine nature, busy yourself with what is creaturely?" If the ground in the depth of the soul has been prepared by man, then, without doubt, God must fill it wholly, or sooner the heavens would burst and fill the void. Still less does God leave anything empty, so contrary is this to His nature and to His ordinance.

And therefore you should observe silence! In that manner the Word can be uttered and heard within. For surely, if you choose to speak, God must fall silent. There is no better way of serving the Word than by silence and by listening. If you go out of yourself, you may be certain that God will enter and fill you wholly: the greater the void, the greater the divine influx.

This exodus is elucidated by a parable from the First Book of Moses. God commanded Abraham to go out of his land and leave his kin, so that He might show him all good. "All good" signifies the divine birth, which contains all good within itself. Land and earth He bade him to leave stand for the body with its worldly gratifications and disorders. By kin we understand the inclinations of our sensual nature and all they entail. They, too, fascinate us and slow down the soul's progress, causing love and grief, pleasure and sorrow, desire and fear, anxiety and frivolity. These inclinations are indeed our close kin, and for that reason we ought to watch them carefully, so that we can turn our back on them completely should the highest good, the divine birth be effected in us.

A proverb says that a child kept too much at home remains uncouth abroad. That holds true of those people who have never left the house of their natural inclinations, who have not gone beyond their nature or beyond all those messages they have received from seeing and hearing, from emotions and excitements. Such people, who have never moved away from sensible things and have never risen above them, will indeed be uncouth when brought face-to-face with divine things. Their interior ground resembles an iron mountain never touched by a ray of light. Once their momentary mood and external circumstances change, such people are at their wits' end. They have never overcome their natural selves and so cannot experience this noble birth. Christ had them in mind when He said: "Whoever leaves father and mother and all possessions for my sake shall receive a hundredfold and eternal life."

Until now we have spoken of the first and the last birth, and how the first should teach us about the last. But now we would like to also refer to the second birth, when God's Son was born on this night of the Mother and has become our brother. In eternity He was born without a mother, and in time He was born without a father. "Mary," so Saint Augustine tells us, "was more blessed because God was born spiritually in her soul than because He was born from her in the flesh." Now whoever wishes this birth to occur in his soul as nobly and as spiritually as it did in Mary's should reflect on the qualities which made her a mother both in spirit and in the flesh. She was a pure maiden, a virgin; she was bethrothed, given in marriage; and she was turned inward, secluded from exterior things, when the Angel came to her. And these are the qualities a spiritual mother ought to possess, should God be born in her soul.

First, the soul should be a pure and chaste virgin. And if it ever lost its purity, it should reverse its ways and become pure and virginal again. It should be a virgin, bringing forth no outward fruit (in the eyes of the world), but much fruit within. This also means shutting out external concerns, not paying too much attention to them, not expecting much reward from them. Mary's heart was fixed solely on the divine. Inwardly a virgin should bear much fruit, for "all the splendor of the King's daughter is within." Thus she should live detached from the exterior world and from the senses. Her conduct, her thoughts, her manner, should all be interiorized. In this way she brings forth great and rich fruit. And this fruit is God Himself, His Son and Word, He Who embraces and contains all that is.

Secondly, Mary was bethrothed; and so should we be, according to Saint Paul's teaching. We should immerse our mutable will into the divine, immutable one, so that our weakness may be turned into strength.

Thirdly, Mary was also turned inward, and if God is to be truly born in us, we must imitate her in this as well and live secluded from the world. This does not come about by merely avoiding temporal distractions which may appear harmful, but, above all, by interiorizing all our acts of virtue. What is truly needful is the creation of inner stillness and peace, a retreat protecting us from our senses, a refuge of tranquillity and inward repose.

This will be the subject of next Sunday's Mass when we sing the Entrance Hymn: "While all things were in quiet silence, and the night was in the midst of its course, Your almighty Word, O Lord, came down from Heaven, out of Your royal throne." And in this nocturnal silence, in which all things remain hushed and in perfect stillness, God's Word is heard in truth, for, should God speak, you must be silent; should He enter, created things must give way.

When Our Lord entered Egypt, all the idols crashed to the ground; those are our false gods, everything that hinders the immediate generation of the divine Word in the soul, however good and holy it may seem. Our Lord tells us that he had come to bring a sword to cut off all that clings to man, even mother, sister, and brother. For that with which you keep intimate company (without God), that is hostile to you. The multiplicity of images conceals the divine Word and prevents its birth in you, although the inner stillness may not be entirely removed. Though it may sometimes desert you, it should nevertheless become a fertile ground for the divine birth. Cherish this deep silence within, nourish it frequently, so that it may become a habit, and by becoming a habit, a mighty possession. For what seems quite impossible to an unpracticed person becomes easy to a practiced one. It is habit which creates skill.

May God help us to prepare a dwelling place for this noble birth, so that we may all attain spiritual motherhood.

AMEN.

SERMON 2

[EVE OF EPIPHANY]

Accipe puerum et matrem eius et vade in terram Israel. . .
Take the child and His mother, and go into the land of
Israel (Mt 2:19)

This Sermon from the Gospel of Saint Matthew falls on the
twelfth eve in Christmastide and deals with the fear of Joseph and the death of Archelaus. It teaches us not to em-
bark hastily on a venture without first considering how it
can be carried through. It also warns of three enemies that
lie in wait for the soul.

No matter how often one may read the glorious words of the
Holy Gospels, preach from them, or meditate on them, one
will always be struck by a new truth that went unnoticed before.
"Take the Child and His mother, and go into the land of Israel, for
they are dead that sought the life of the Child."

As soon as some people feel an aspiration for a renewal of their
interior life, their enthusiasm carries them away. They become so
impetuous about the newness of it all that they never stop to wonder
if they perhaps take on more than they can manage, or if God's grace
in them is such that they can carry it through. One should always
consider the end before one hastily embarks on a new devotion. The
first thing is to have recourse to God and commend to Him one's new
spiritual fervor and impetus. But this is not the way some people
choose; they want to rush off by themselves and start all kinds of new
practices, and in their rashness they come to grief, because they rely
on their strength alone.

When Joseph had fled into Egypt with the Child and His
mother, and an Angel had told him in his dream that Herod was

41

dead, he greatly feared that the Child would be killed, because he learned that Herod's son Archelaus was now on the throne. Herod, who wanted to persecute the Child and kill Him, signifies the world, which would doubtless kill the Child, and we must certainly flee from it if we wish to retain the Child within us. But even when we have fled the world, in an exterior sense, and have retired into our cells and cloisters, there will always be an Archelaus reigning in the soul. A whole world will rise up in us which we will never overcome without constant practice and effort and the help of God. There are strong and fierce foes which will assail us, and to vanquish them is exceedingly hard.

First there is worldliness and spiritual pride. You wish to be seen and noticed and highly thought of; you want to impress others with your appearance and grand manner; you desire to be known for your brilliant talk, your worldly ways, your friends, family, wealth, rank, and all the rest. The second enemy is your own flesh, which attacks you with spiritual impurity; for a person is guilty of this whenever he indulges in sensual satisfactions, no matter of what kind they may be. Everybody has different temptations against impurity and he should guard carefully against them. Some people have a tendency toward infatuations of one kind or another, and they cherish them willfully in their hearts, day in and day out. For just as your bodily nature can lead your body to impurity, so your inward impurity takes away the noble purity of the spirit; and since your spirit is far nobler than your flesh, the sins of the spirit are also graver and more grievous. Your third enemy is malice, resentment, suspiciousness, rash judgment, feelings of hatred and spite. "Do you know what this person has done? And what he has said about me?" you say, and your bitter gestures, words, and actions make it clear that you will pay back the offender in any possible way. You may be convinced that all this is the work of the devil.

If you wish to be pleasing to God, you must renounce all this sort of thing, for it is the veritable work of Archelaus. Beware of this enemy, for it is he who can kill the Child for you.

But Joseph was constantly on his guard against anyone who might seek to kill the Child. In the same way, even when all the enemies are overcome, there are still a thousand ties to break. Only if you turn inward and look into your heart can you tell what they are. "Joseph" means a constant growth in the interior life and an active progress in spiritual things. They are indeed the best guard for the Child and His Mother.

Joseph was warned by the Angel and called back by him to the land of Israel. Now, Israel means land of vision. At this point many spiritual-minded people go astray, for they want to free themselves from their innumerable ties without waiting for God to set them free by the sending of His Angel. Thus they fall into grievous error. They want to free themselves with the aid of their cleverness and their ability to hold forth about such lofty matters as the Blessed Trinity. It is a great pity to think what harm and misunderstanding this has caused, and still causes every day. Such people refuse to endure the chains of captivity in the darkness which is Egypt, for Egypt means darkness. One thing you may be sure of: No creature God has ever called into life can free you or help you. God alone can do it. Run about as you will, search the whole world, you will never find the help you need except in God. If God wishes to avail Himself of an instrument, man or Angel, to achieve His purpose, He may do so, but nonetheless it is He Who does the work. Therefore you should look into the depth of your soul, and give up all the running and outward searching; patiently endure, surrender yourself to God, and remain in the darkness of Egypt until the Angel comes to call you.

Joseph was asleep when the warning came. A person asleep does not sin, even if some evil thought comes to him, provided he has not caused it previously. In the same manner we should be asleep to all exterior sufferings and temptations which may assail us. We should accept them with calm endurance, humbly submitting ourselves to God, as if we were asleep and cared for nothing. This attitude of self-surrender to the End is the best safeguard against sin. In this sleep, in that true passivity, you will hear the calling of the voice.

Such guardians the prelates of the Church should be: Pope and bishops, abbots, priors and prioresses, and father confessors, too. They should all be guardians of the young, each one guarding them in the way that will benefit them most. All of us have many guardians, many superiors. I have a prior, a provincial, a master-general, a pope, a bishop. All of these are my superiors. And if they all turned upon me as ferociously as wolves, I should submit, I hope, with true humility. If they were benevolent and kind, I should accept that, too. And if they wanted to do me harm, and if there were a hundred times as many of them as there are now, I ought to suffer it all with equal resignation.

Note that Joseph was in constant fear, although the Angel announced that those who sought the Child's life were dead; he diligently inquired who reigned in the land of Israel. There are those who want to live free from all fear. This is wrong, for as long as you live on this earth you will never be free from fear. "*Timor sanctus permanet in saeculum saeculi*"—"the fear of the Lord shall remain until the end of the world." Even if an Angel came and spoke to you, you should still be afraid and inquire diligently who is really reigning in you. Somewhere Archelaus may still be in power.

Joseph took the Child and His mother. By the Child we should understand a spotless purity. We should remain unstained by transitory things, and small like a child in submission and humility. By the mother we should understand a true love of God, for love is the mother of true humility; it is love which makes our self-will decrease so that we become childlike in pure submission to God's will. While man is still young he should not stray into the land of vision at will; he may do so to ask pardon, but then he must return to Egypt again. Let him stay there till he has grown to full manhood, steeled by the weapons of Our Lord Jesus Christ. He has taught us everything by His example; anything we are not told explicitly may be learned from His life. When He was twelve years old, He came to Jerusalem, but He did not remain there; He withdrew because He had not reached full manhood. He withdrew till He reached the age of thirty, He was there every day, rebuking and admonishing the Jews and teaching the truth as a master. He preached and instructed them, dwelling in the countryside, going wherever He wished, to Capernaum and Galilee and Nazareth, and all through Judea. He was a mighty teacher, working signs and wonders.

In this manner we, too, should act: As long as we are children and imperfect, we should not settle in that noble land, the land of the Lord; we may go there from time to time for a fleeting visit and then return again. But when we have reached full manhood we may come and live in the land of Judea. "Juda" means "to confess God." We can teach and admonish now, in the true peace, which is Jerusalem, and then cross over to Galilee; it is indeed a crossing over. For here all things have been overcome, and by this transcending Nazareth is reached, the sweet flower-garden where the blossoms of eternal life abound and where we experience a true foretaste of it. Here is utter security, inexpressible peace, tranquillity, and joy. We arrive there only by waiting in patience and submission for God to lead us forth. Those who have thus surrendered their will shall enter this peace, this blossoming of Nazareth, and here we shall find what will be our everlasting joy.

May God in His loving bounty grant us to share in this.

AMEN.

SERMON 5
[FEAST OF EPIPHANY II]

Surge et illuminare, Ierusalem . . .
Rise up, Jerusalem, and shine forth . . . (Is 60:1)

This is a second Sermon for the Twelfth Day in Christmastide. The theme is taken from the Epistle of the Day
(Is 51:17, 52:2), which teaches us to abandon ourselves and
all created things so that God may find the ground prepared in which to accomplish His eternal work.

"Rise up, Jerusalem and shine forth!" God desires and needs
only one thing in all the world; and that He desires so ardently that He sets His whole heart upon it. It is this: to find the
lofty ground with which He had endowed man's spirit empty and
prepared so that He may accomplish His eternal work within it.
God, Who is all-powerful in Heaven and on Earth, asks for man's
consent to bring this about. What, then, ought we to do so that God
may shine forth in this very sweet ground of the soul and perform
His work there? We should rise, "surge." The text says arise, which
implies an active consent. Man must do his part and rise from everything that is not God, away from himself and all created things. And
as he rises, the depth of his soul is seized by a powerful longing to
be denuded and freed from everything that separates it from God.
And the more he leaves behind all that is finite, the stronger his longing grows, it transcends itself, and when this denuded ground is
touched, the desire often overflows into flesh and blood and bone.

There are two kinds of people, who react differently when
touched by this desire. The first approach it with natural reason,
with images borrowed from it, and with high speculations. Thus
they bring confusion to this depth. They stifle this desire by trying

to understand what is happening to their souls. They derive a certain peace from their efforts, but it is an illusory peace. They think they are Jerusalem. Some of them follow their own ideas and choose their own techniques in prayer and meditation, or perhaps imitate what other people are doing. They believe that in this way they are preparing the ground of their souls and they expect to find peace. It seems to them that they have already become "Jerusalem." They insist on their method and they will not hear of another. But, alas, it is a false peace, for such people persist in their same old faults: be it pride, attachment to physical comforts, gratification afforded by the senses and other created things. They still make uncharitable judgments and at the slightest provocation they lash out in hatred against their neighbor. Their peace is a fraudulent one, for by keeping their own counsel they have not arisen and God cannot therefore work in them. They have to abandon their presumptions and arrogant ways and begin the strenuous work of self-denial, following the steps of Our Lord Jesus Christ in humility and love. By dying to self they have to learn what it means to truly arise.

On the other hand, we encounter noble souls so steeped in truth that it shines forth in them. They permit God to prepare the ground, leaving themselves entirely to Him. By this act of self-surrender they refuse to cling to anything of their own, be it their works, their special devotions, what they undertake and what they leave aside. They accept all things from God in humble awe and refer them back to Him in total detachment, bowing lowly to the divine Will. Whatever God may send, they are well pleased to accept it. Peace or strife are all one to them. Of such people one may well say what the Lord said to the disciples when they went up to Jerusalem: "Go up, your time is always here, but my time has not yet come." Their time is forever the same for they are unencumbered and surrendered to God's will; His time, however, is not known. Whenever it is that He may deign to come with His divine illumination, they await Him with sweet patience.

How different are these people who allow God to prepare the ground. They do not take matters into their own hands. Yet for all that, they, too, are prone to temptation, for no one is exempt from that. However, when tempted, through pride or carnal desire, through wordly attachments, anger, or whatever else, they immediately surrender it all to God and they allow themselves to fall into His loving arms. Such people do indeed rise up, for they go beyond themselves. They become a true Jerusalem; they dwell in peace in the midst of strife, and they possess joy in sorrow. Whatever God may ordain, they accept it with joy, and the whole world cannot deprive them of such serenity. If man and all the devils in hell had sworn to rob them of their peace, they could not do it. Their gaze is fixed unswervingly on God and they are truly filled with light, for God's light is pure and radiant everywhere, but nowhere does it shine brighter than in the deepest darkness. Ah, how glorious such men are! They are raised to a supernatural, a divine level, and none of their work is ever done without God. And if one may dare to utter it, they themselves no longer work, but God works in them. How blessed they are! They are the lofty pillars of the universe, on whom rests the weight of the whole world. To find oneself in such a state— what a glorious and joyful thing that would be.

The difference between the two kinds of people is this: The first want to prepare the depths of their souls themselves and will not leave it to God. Their faculties are imprisoned in their sins, from which they cannot free themselves. They may even delight in persisting in them of their own free will.

The others, however, those noble souls who allow God to do His work in them, those blessed men who have died to themselves and to the world, they are now lifted high above themselves. As soon as they are assailed by sin and become aware of it, they flee unto God and there can be no more trace of sin, for they now dwell in God's freedom.

External works are of no avail to them, of none whatsoever. Does not the word "surge" mean arise? That indeed is a work. It is the one work necessary, and they should perform it without ceasing as long as they live. A man can never reach perfection unless he wishes to arise, lift up his spirit to God, and free his innermost ground. Always and everywhere he ought to ask: "Where is He who has been born?" (Mt 2:2). He should do this with profound awe and with inward recollection, so that he may fully know what God wishes him to do. If He sends sufferings to such people, they will suffer them; if He demands good works, they will perform them; and if He sends sweet joys, they will rejoice in them. Their ground bears witness to Him who prepared and purified it. God is the sole ruler of this innermost depth of the soul and no creature must ever enter it.

God works through indirect means within the first kind of people, but in the second kind, in these noble and blessed souls, He works directly, without means. But what it is that He does in those depths of the soul which have been touched by Him directly, no one can say. Nor can any man tell another, and even he who has experienced it must remain silent. For where God truly takes possession of the soul, all external activity ceases, but the interior perception of God mightily increases. Once a man has attained such a height to which God's grace and his own ardor have brought him, he must deny himself utterly, according to Our Lord's words: "We are servants, and worthless; it was our duty to do what we have done" (Lk 17:10). Never can a man reach such perfection that he would not have to remain in awesome fear. Even if he reaches the very highest peak he is to say and mean: "*Fiat voluntas tua*"—"Lord, thy will be done." Let him keep guard over himself lest he have any hidden attachments, so that God should find in his innermost ground an obstacle that would prevent Him from this work He performs so loftily and without means. May our loving God help us to "rise up," so that He may accomplish His work within us.

AMEN.

SERMON 10
[FIFTH SATURDAY IN LENT]

Ego sum lux mundi, dicit Dominus
I am the light of the world, says the Lord (Jn 8:12)

This Sermon for the Fifth Saturday in Lent takes its text from the Gospel of Saint John. It urges us to return to our origin, and points out the obstacles that keep us from doing so. It also draws a distinction between the true lovers of God and the false ones.

Our Lord said: "I am the light of the world." The Jews responded to this by saying that He came from Galilee and therefore He was the concern of the Galileans, not theirs. His answer to that was: "I am the light of the whole world and of all men." And from this light which leads all creatures back to their origin, all other light derives: Every earthly light derives from it, as sun, moon, and stars, and the eyes of men; and every spiritual light, too, as the light of human intellect. And whenever the created light is not referred back to the uncreated one, it is in itself darkness, in opposition to the true essential light which enlightens the whole world. Now our dear Lord said: "Abandon your own light which is really darkness, opposed to My light, and transform yourself into darkness; then I shall give you My external light so that it may be yours as it is Mine, My being and life, My bliss and joy." In the same manner He prayed to His Father, "that they may be one as We are one, I in You and You in Me; thus not just joined together but wholly one, that they may be one with Us," not by nature but, incomprehensibly, by grace.

We know that all the elements possess an inherent tendency to return to their natural place of origin. This is true of every created thing; stones must fall; fire must rise. Surely the same should be true of man, God's noble creation, the marvel of all God's marvelous works, for whom He created all the rest, heaven and earth and everything that He made. How could man alone be so self-absorbed and not rush back to his eternal source, his goal and his light?

There are two things to be considered here: first, how man should return to his source, the road he should travel, and the means he should use to arrive at his goal; second, the obstacles which prevent him from achieving his goal. Formidable indeed must be the obstacles which can keep him back and turn him from his path when he is pursuing a good so unutterably high.

Two different types of people are hindered by two different obstacles. There are those whose hearts are worldly and they seek pleasure and satisfaction in their senses and in created things. They waste away their faculties and their senses, and all their time is occupied with such matters. They live entirely in darkness and represent the opposite of this light.

Then there are the others, who are devoted to religious life and enjoy great esteem and reputation. They are pretty sure that they have left the darkness far behind; and yet they are fundamentally Pharisees, filled with self-love and self-will. All their striving is centered upon themselves. Outwardly one can barely tell them from God's friends, for they often spend more time on pious exercises than God's friends: One can always see them reciting prayers, keeping fasts and strict rules. If judged by externals, they are hard to recognize. But those in whom God's Spirit dwells know them for what they are. In fact, even outwardly there is a way of distinguishing them: They are always sitting in judgment upon others, also upon those who love God: but you never see them judging themselves, whereas the true lovers of God judge no one but themselves. In everything, in God and in His creatures, such people seek nothing but their own gratification. So deeply embedded is this pharisaical tendency in their nature that every corner of the soul is invaded by it. It is impossible to overcome this habit by natural means; one might as well break down mountains of iron. There is only one way, and that is for God to take over and inhabit man. And this He does only for those who love Him.

Alas, the world is filled with such self-seeking, and wherever one turns one sees no end to the trouble it causes. It is enough to dry up and chill the hearts of God's lovers, to observe so many people doing such great injustice to their God by acting in such a perilous way.

When we consider all this, it becomes clear that a great spiritual effort is required. As long as we live, we need to fight against self-love, for it will never be completely conquered. It is indeed a formidable obstacle, which hinders us from finding the true light and from returning to this source. Wherever such an inclination prevails, people will try to adhere to their own natural light, for the light of natural reason confers such great satisfaction that the pleasures of the world are as nothing compared to it. Even pagans have realized this: By clinging to this natural light and not going beyond it, they were bound to remain in everlasting darkness. Such, then, are the obstacles which prevent us from finding the true light.

Now we must put our mind to finding the right mode, the straight and shortest path that leads to this origin and to this true light. We arrive at it by genuine self-denial and by meaning and loving only God, utterly and completely. Not our own, but God's glory and honor. We must intend and seek everything from Him alone, without compromise. We must offer everything back to Him directly and not in a roundabout way, so that a free-flowing passage may be created, along which He can come to us and we to Him: This is the true, straight way.

It is the watershed which separates God's true friends from the false ones. The false ones refer everything to themselves instead of referring God's gifts back to Him in purity of intention, in love and gratitude, in total surrender and forgetfulness of self. This is the mark of the true friend of God. Whoever does not seek and possess this mark and who, at the hour of death, persists in his self-absorption will never see the true light. How alarming and ruinous such a course is: Without realizing it, one has found only nature where one had hoped to find God.

Grievous sufferings, too, make us aware whether we possess the true love of God or not. God's true friends take refuge in Him and accept all sorrow freely for His sake, thus suffering with Him and in Him. Or they lose themselves in Him in such a loving union that suffering ceases to be felt as such and turns into joy. For those whose spirit is false, it is quite otherwise. When afflicted with sorrow, they do not know which way to turn; they run this way and that, looking for help and advice and comfort, and when they do not find it, they break down and fall into despair. It is very doubtful what their last hours will be like, for they cannot find God within their inmost ground. They have not built their house upon Christ, who is the cornerstone, and thus they are bound to plunge into the abyss.

Such people are a thousand times more to be pitied than ordinary worldlings who consider themselves wicked and live in humble fear as did the ordinary people who followed Our Lord in His lifetime. It was the Pharisees, the high priests and scribes who opposed Him and brought about His death, although on the surface they appeared to be holy men. One can say nothing to such people; they will either fight or flee, as they did when Christ wrote upon the ground. They refused to admit their failings, and it was the learned and the elders who turned away first, until every one of them had gone (Jn 8:1). It is far easier to help and advise the simple, because they do admit their failings and one can give good counsel to those who consider themselves sinful and who live in fear and humility.

To overcome these various obstacles, our loving God has lent us great help and comfort: He sent His only-begotten Son, so that His holy life and His great and perfect virtue, His example and teaching, and His manifold suffering should draw us out of ourselves, and that we should extinguish our own dark light in His true, essential light. He gave us the holy sacraments: first, baptism and holy chrism, then, should we fall from grace, confession and penance. He gave us His blessed Body and, at the hour of death, holy unction.

Strong indeed are the remedies and supports which are to bring us back to our origin and to our beginning. Saint Augustine says: "The great sun has created for itself a lesser sun, and veiled it into a cloud, not to render it invisible, but to temper its brightness, so that we should be able to glance at it." The great sun is our heavenly Father, Who brought forth a lesser sun, which is the Son. And although the Son is equal to the Father by His divinity, He made Himself less than the Father by His humanity, not to hide Himself, but to temper His brightness for us, so that we may be able to behold Him. "For He is the true light which enlightens every man who comes into the world."

"This light shines in the darkness, but the darkness has not comprehended it." No one receives it but the poor in spirit who have stripped themselves of self-love and self-will. There are many who have lived for forty years in material poverty without having ever beheld this light. They understand what it is, they have taken it in with their senses and grasped it with their intellect, but in the depth of their souls it is alien and repugnant to them.

My Beloved, strive with all your might, with every effort of body and soul, to behold this true light, so that you may be able to return to the source where it shines in all its brightness. Long for it, pray for it, do all that you can, with all the strength you can summon. Entreat those who love God to help you. Cling to those who cling to God, so that they may draw you with them into God. May our loving God help us to attain this.

AMEN.

SERMON 11
[MONDAY BEFORE PALM SUNDAY]

Si quis sitit, veniat et bibat . . .
If any man thirst, let him come to Me and drink . . .
(Jn 7:37)

This Sermon, preached on Monday before Palm Sunday, deals with the Passion of Our Lord according to Saint John. It speaks of the soul's loving thirst for God, and shows how man is pursued by the hounds of his manifold temptations.

On the last day of a great feast, Our Lord cried out with a loud voice. "If any man thirst, let him come to me and drink." We are approaching the time of the precious Passion of Our Lord, and no man should let it pass without feeling in his heart great sorrow and compassion and gratitude. And furthermore, since God, Our Sovereign Lord and Father, suffered such great indignities and so many torments, all those who would like to be counted among His friends should be glad to suffer with Him, whether they have deserved it or not. They should rejoice that they are given the honor and joy of being like Him by following His footsteps.

"If any man thirst," what does this signify? When the Holy Spirit comes into our souls, He causes a burning love, a flaming love which sets the soul on fire. The heat flashes off sparks and this engenders a thirst for God and a loving desire. Sometimes a man does not know what is happening to him, so overcome is he by sadness and disgust for created things. The desire is threefold, and it occurs in three different kinds of people, who differ greatly from each other. The first are beginners, the second are those who have made some

55

progress, and the third may be called perfect, as far as perfection is possible in this world.

Saint David said in the Psalms: "Just as the hart thirsts for the stream, so my soul thirsts for you, O Lord." The hart is hunted across woods and hills, till the great heat of the chase causes an intense thirst, and he longs for water more eagerly than any other animal. Just as the hart is hunted by hounds, so men who are beginners in the spiritual life are pursued by temptations as soon as they turn away from the world. They are particularly pursued by their great and grave sins. These are the seven deadly ones, and they hunt the soul with strong and violent temptations, far worse than anything it had known when still in the world. Before, the soul was barely conscious of temptation; how, however, it is aware of being hunted. Thus Solomon said: "My son, when you enter into God's service, prepare your heart at once to resist temptation." The harder and fiercer the chase, the more intense our thirst for God ought to become. Now it may happen occasionally that one of the hounds will overtake the hart and seize it by the belly with its teeth. When the hart tries to shake itself free of the hound, he will drag it to a tree, dash it against the trunk and crush its head to be freed. This is just the way we should act. If we find that we cannot overcome the hounds, our temptations, we should run with great haste to the Tree of the Cross and Passion of Our Lord Jesus Christ, and thus crush the head of the hound which is our temptation. In this way we should overcome the whole lot of them, and be freed of them at once.

However, when the hart has overcome the big hounds, the little ones come running around, snapping at him. He takes hardly any notice of them, yet they maul him badly and do him genuine harm. The same happens to us: When we have conquered and overcome our grave sins, we take no notice of the little hounds which signify superficial concerns, frivolous occupations, and all such trivialities. These things take little bites out of us, distracting our hearts and stifling true inwardness; they weaken the divine life within the soul to such an extent that in the end grace and love begin to seriously diminish. And so we come to lose the fervor that draws us to God, and both awe and adoration begin to pale. These little temptations are far more dangerous than the great ones. Aware of their evil, we are on guard against them, but the petty flaws hardly seem worth our attention. Nevertheless, that which we cannot recognize as bad is far more pernicious than that which we can; and so it is with these worldly occupations, with frivolities and vanities to which we pay no heed.

After the hart has felt the heat of the chase, his thirst begins to increase. And this is the way we ought to act when we are pressed hard by temptation: We should experience a strong attraction, a thirsting after God, Who alone is our truth and peace, our justice and comfort.

Once the hart is overcome by thirst and fatigue, the huntsmen often feed the hounds a little in order to hold them back. They want to give the hart a chance to cool off so that he can face the chase with renewed strength. Our Lord deals with us in a familiar way: As soon as He perceives that the temptations and the pressures overwhelm us, He delays them and distills a delectable drop into our hearts, a foretaste of the divine sweetness. This strengthens us mightily, so much so that all things which are not God lose their attraction, and it seems to us that we have overcome all danger. But this respite was only meant to infuse us with renewed vigor in order to meet the oncoming challenge. And just when we least expect it, the hounds pursue us as fiercely as they did before. Only now we are strengthened and better able to defend ourselves.

All this God permits to happen because of His great care and love for us. He allows the soul to be hard pressed, till there is no other path open to it but God, in Whom rests all peace and truth and consolation. He permits this, so that the drink which quenches our thirst may taste all the sweeter and more delectable, now and throughout eternity. There we shall drink gladly from the sweetest of all fountains, in long drafts, from the fountainhead which is God's paternal heart. And in this life it gives us good comfort, and it enables us to deem all trials small, as long as they are borne for the sake of God.

When the hart has escaped from all the hounds and reaches the water, he drinks his fill without restraint. And this is just what we do when, with the help of Our Lord, we have shaken off all these hounds, both big and small, and we come thirsting to God. What should we do now? We draw in as much as we can of this divine draft, and we become so filled with God that we forget ourselves in this overflowing bliss. We think that we are capable of wonders, that we could gladly pass through fire and water and a thousand swords.

Neither life nor death do we fear and joy and sorrow are the same to us. We have become inebriated, a state known as "jubilation." Sometimes a man in such a state will cry aloud, or sing or laugh.

Now along come reasonable people, ignorant of the wondrous ways of the Holy Spirit, ignorant of everything outside the natural order. "Merciful heavens," they exclaim, "why are you carrying on in this ridiculous manner?" They do not see God's hand in it. This state is followed by an unutterable joy; whatever happens to such people, whatever is done to them, it fills them with true peace and delectation, for love is aflame in them, and it glimmers and glows and consumes them with bliss.

There is a third state, in which a man may die of a broken heart because God works in him so strongly and vehemently that it is more than he can bear. You should know that many a man has died of this, giving himself up so utterly to these wondrously great works that his nature could not endure it and collapsed under the strain.

When our dear Lord sees that people allow themselves to be thus overcome, and are drowning in their experience, He behaves like a good head of the family who has laid down plenty of good wine; while he was asleep, his children have gone down to the cellar and made themselves drunk. When the father awakens and sees what has happened, he cuts himself a strong stick and thrashes the children thoroughly, so that they are as miserable now as they were happy before. Then he gives them enough water to drink to make them as sober as they were drunk. This is the way the Lord proceeds: He acts as if He were asleep, and lets his friends take from His riches as much as they want. But when He sees that this is no longer to their advantage, and that they have taken on more than they can bear, He withdraws the emotional comforts, their strong wine, and allows them to grow as sad as they were joyful, as sober as they were drunk before. And their experience of joy begins to fade away.

Alas, what good is it to them now, to have been so drunk? When they were thirsty, they were given all the drink they needed. In doing this, the Lord drew them on and out of themselves, freeing them of the miseries captive creatures are prone to. But since they have lost all restraint, He wishes to recall them to sobriety. They are now sober and prudent, seeing themselves for what they are and realizing what they are capable of. Whereas they performed everything in excess before, they now observe moderation. Being left to their own resources they can barely do the slightest work without great difficulty, and the least word of criticism is more than they can bear. But they have learned what their capabilities and limitations really are, and this makes them calm, sober, and at peace.

Even so, this whole process with its tempestuous emotions has taken place in the lower faculties, where God will never make His home. It is not His proper dwelling-place; it is too narrow and too confined and leaves Him no room to move about so that He may achieve His glorious work. He wishes to dwell, He will dwell only in man's higher faculties; there alone will He perform His unique work. There alone, where He recognizes His own image and likeness, will He make His abode. And whoever wishes to find God in truth must seek Him there and nowhere else.

Whoever arrives here has discovered what he has been searching for far and wide. His spirit will be led into a hidden desert far beyond his natural faculties. Words cannot describe it, for it is the unfathomable darkness where the divine Goodness reigns above all distinctions. And the soul is led further, into the oneness of God's simple unity, so that it loses the ability to draw any distinctions between the object and its own emotions. For in this unity all multiplicity is lost; it is the unity which unifies multiplicity.

When such a man returns to himself, his perception will be clearer and more wonderful than before, for it has arisen from unity and simplicity. He now can perceive the distinctions relating to the Articles of his Faith—how Father, Son, and Holy Spirit are one God—indeed relating to all truth. No one can understand these distinctions better than those who have gone beyond distinctions and have attained unity. This state is called and indeed is an unfathomable darkness, and yet it is the essential light. It is and is said to be an incomprehensible and solitary wilderness, for no one can find his way there, for it is above all ways, above all modes and manners.

This "darkness" is to be understood in such a way: It is a light inaccessible to created reason, far beyond its comprehension. It is a wilderness because no natural path leads to it. In this wilderness the spirit is raised above itself, above all its powers of comprehension and understanding, and the soul now drinks from the very spring, from the true and essential source. How sweet and fresh and pure are the waters at the source, before they have lost their freshness as they flow on into the riverbed. Oh, what a delectable and pure stream the soul receives from this source! With all its powers the soul lets itself sink deep into these waters. It longs to take even deeper drafts, but this cannot happen as long as it is in this world. The soul sinks into the depth of the ground and loses itself there just as a stream trickles over the ground and seeps into it.

Now if a man, as soon as he has reached this summit, falls back into inactivity on the level of his lower powers, and allows the higher ones to lie dormant, his aspirations will come to nothing. The lower faculties must be put in their place if spiritual pride and license are not to take over. Such a person will remain in a state of complacency and persevere in his old habits, and nothing will come of him. Rather he should submit in profound humility to the will of God. God now expects a more radical detachment from all that is finite, a greater purity of intention, a stripping of all creatureliness, an unencumbered and single-minded spirit, an inward and outward stillness. This state will then lead to intimacy with God and finally to a blessed mode of being.

Do you now perceive what all this means? Have you understood how God leads the soul along wondrous paths, and how He reveals Himself in His works? How at first the soul took onto itself what was His alone, and how it was lost because it could not possess what was God's? How the soul became disconsolate, disordered, and unsettled? Now, however, the soul is led to a blessed state in which it is raised high above itself and all its powers. Now it is God Who surrenders Himself to the soul, altogether different from before, so that it is well ordered in sweet harmony. Thus the Beloved in the Song of Songs says: "*Introduxit me rex in cellarium*"—to his own cellar the King has brought me and there he has truly ordered that love.

Indeed, He has truly ordered that love; He has led the Beloved along wondrous and awesome paths into the innermost abyss which is He Himself. What the soul encounters there soars above all the senses. Reason may not touch it, no one may grasp or understand it, it is a true foretaste of eternal life.

Behold how God's loving goodness has His sweet sport with those He has chosen for Himself. He longs ardently that we should come to Him and that we should thirst for Him, and hence He called with a strong voice: "If any man thirst, let him come to me and drink!" So strongly does He long for this thirst of ours, so ardent is His desire to satisfy it, that the bodies of those who partake of this drink will overflow with living waters which stream forth into eternal life.

What are we to understand by "body"? Just as the body enjoys and receives and distributes our earthly food so that every member and the entire body are equally strengthened by it, so the spirit receives this lofty drink which then is diffused by God's loving ardor into all the members, into our entire life and being, so that all our actions are better ordered, ordered in perfect harmony. And as the interior order is reflected in the outer man, he will flourish and wax and grow into God's will, and so continue into eternal life. May God help us that we may all share in this.

AMEN.

SERMON 18
[ASCENSION I]

Recumbentibus undecim discipulis
When the eleven disciples were sitting together . . .
(Mk 16:14)

The first interpretation of Our Lord's Ascension speaks of certain people whom God upbraided for their incredulity and hardness of heart. He thoroughly condemns their superficial concerns and compares them to cisterns full of putrid water.

W hen Our Lord's disciples were sitting together, the Lord Jesus appeared to them and rebuked them for their lack of faith and hardness of heart.

Our Lord is still making this reproach every day and every hour because of the unbelief and hardheartedness of people in all states of life. He particularly reproaches religious, whether they are members of canonically instituted orders or congregations such as Beguines or Sisters and others. These Our Lord rebukes sometimes through their teachers and sometimes by speaking to them in their own hearts, if they are indeed ready to listen.

Religious are to be blamed in a very grievous manner if they are guilty of hardheartedness and unbelief. It is after all an extraordinary and lofty thing that God should have elected and called them to the religious life. Hence they owe God an extraordinary and surpassing love, a boundless gratitude. Such people Our Lord reproves for being faithless and hardhearted. If only they could bring themselves to accept reproof, recognize these faults, and confess their guilt, then perhaps a remedy could be found.

Saint James teaches that faith without works is dead. And

Christ says that he who believes and is baptized shall be saved. We all proclaim our faith by mouth. What are Saint Paul's words? "All we who are baptized in Christ Jesus are baptized in His death." And Saint Augustine teaches: "That is not true faith that does not hasten to God with living love and good works, but is only proclaimed by mouth." Unbelief, in this sense, is clearly shown when we are attracted by created things or desire them instead of saying: "Lord, You are my God, and my happiness rests in You alone." To think otherwise is to have fallen away from the true, living faith. I am speaking particularly of those who have a reputation for spirituality and who have in the past perhaps known the touch or the finger of God in the depths of their hearts, consciously or unconsciously, and now have fallen away from all this.

Our Lord reproves these people for hardness of heart. It is an awful thing that those whom God has specially called to Himself have grown so indifferent that divine things have lost their appeal for them, whether prayer or any other good practice. Other things give them great pleasure, but toward God their hearts are of stone. Our Lord had them in mind when He spoke through the Prophet Ezekiel: "I will take away your stony heart and will give you a heart of flesh." What is it, then, that makes these hearts so cold and arid that all the good which ought to attract them appears to be so wearisome? Clearly, the heart must cherish something that is not God, its own self or something else. And the trouble is that such people will not accept reproof.

It is to them that Our Lord spoke through the Prophet Jeremiah: "Be astonished, O ye heavens, at this, and ye gates thereof be very desolate, says the Lord. For my people have done two evils. They have forsaken Me, the fountain of living water, and have digged to themselves cisterns, broken cisterns that can hold no water." What comes into a cistern comes from outside or runs from above, as happens with rain or other waters, which become putrid and foul; but there is no water springing up from the ground. God laments of this in the sight of heaven and earth and all creatures and His friends, as of a great evil. Who is this people over whom God laments? It is His own people, those who are in religious states of life. So utterly have they abandoned these life-giving waters that in the depths of their souls there is hardly a flicker of light or life but only superficialities. They perversely cling to their external unspiritual ways and observances; they live from the outside in, relying entirely on sensible images received from without. But within, there is no water springing up from the ground of their souls, none whatsoever.

Surely, these are the cisterns from which nothing wells up from the ground, from which everything flows away as quickly as it came. What may pass for religion in these people is nothing but a set of methods and practices of their own choice. They do not turn to their ground; they have neither desire nor thirst for what is profound and never go below the surface. As long as they have fulfilled their outward observances, they are thoroughly satisfied. The cisterns they have made for themselves suit them fine, and for God they do not thirst. And so they go to sleep at night, and they rise again in the morning to their old routine, with which they are well pleased. But by adhering to the cisterns which they have dug for themselves in such a blind, cold, and hard way, they leave the fountains of living water untouched. Our Lord, however, said: "You have prostituted yourself and made yourself unclean." And in an earlier chapter we read: "All this is because you have forsaken Me, the living fountain, and have digged you a cistern and have forsaken Me."

Whatever collects in these cisterns becomes foul and putrid and dries up. The taste of the living water is not for them; they leave well enough alone. What pertains exclusively to the senses leaves the soul parched. There one finds pride, self-will, hardheartedness, rash judgment, harsh words, bad manners, and reproach of one's neighbor—not a reproach caused by love and concern, but one that is out of place and ill considered. There are plenty of people who think to extinguish the fire in another man's house and burn down their own. And if such rash, destructive people owned three houses, and a poor man came along, they would call him an impostor; and a poor woman they would call a Beguine. What a pity. It is you who are the true cisterns! If the living fountain had ever sprung up in these dry grounds of yours, you would make no such discriminations. There would be no belittling of others, no harsh judgments, no hardness of heart. Such foulness is bred only in cisterns.

It sometimes happens that men of high "culture," with their high-sounding words and sparkling minds, are cisterns like the rest. They are quite pleased with their eminence and with the impression they make all around. How do you think they will fare when the storms of wrath and destruction will sweep over them, when horrible and fearful plagues come upon the earth? Then there will be lamentation beyond belief. People who have lived under the cloak of their celebrity, their brilliance and learning, full of sham holiness, they all were devoid of living faith, frauds and cisterns, and will be prey to the devil in the end. All this he will rend with a single blow of his axe. Immediately it will turn into dust and be scattered away. Every trace will be gone, for there was nothing in the ground. The waters in the cistern were foul. These people wanted to seem rather than to be, whereas they were nothing.

Beloved, when do you believe all this will be clearly seen? Remember what I have told you when you come into the next world. I know perfectly well that pretense and ostentation are common practice among those in religious states of life. Their attitude is superficial, hypocritical, and entirely bound to the senses. They will be far surpassed by people living in the world, in married or widowed state, very far indeed. And if God in His mercy grants these religious to be saved in the end, you may be sure that they will suffer severe and prolonged purgatorial pains according to God's ordinance. And even after that they will find themselves far removed from God's presence.

Beloved, I beseech you, by the love of God, to keep a good watch over yourselves. Be always aware of the ground within your soul, and of what occupies your minds. Be docile, humble, and subject to God and His creatures, for God laments of you to the heavens, to the earth, and to all creatures. The heavens are the heavenly heart, for every good man is a heaven of God, and even those we were speaking of are carrying heaven within them, though they do not enter it. This is the greatest torment of the damned: to know of that heaven within them and yet to be not able to enter it.

We touched upon the words Our Lord spoke through the Prophet Jeremiah: "You have prostituted yourself and followed a stranger as your lover; you have despised Me and gone after a stranger's love; but now come back to Me and I will give you true repentance and pour into you living waters, if only you will return to Me with all your heart."

Observe the inconceivable and inexpressible mercy and goodness of God. How gladly He would help us if we would allow Him to; how gladly He would talk to us as friend speaks to friend if we would only approach Him. As Our Lord said before: "If you fail to come back to Me I will contend with you in judgment." And this is quite a serious contest, for we know He will retain the upper hand.

Take heed, that He will not say that you are not of His sheep.

For His sheep have heard His voice and have not followed a stranger, as He Himself said. What, then, is this prostitution which Our Lord said you committed? According to the spiritual sense, and without interpreting it more coarsely, it is, to say the least, that you have come to a standstill at the world of the senses. And the stranger whom you have followed, this lover of yours, is the multitude of alien images and notions through which you should have passed to Him. With such things you have sullied yourself. But now come to Me: I will receive you and will pour living waters in you.

This water Our Lord mentions in the New Testament on two occasions: "If any man thirst, let him come to Me and drink." "He that believes in me," as Scripture says, "out of his belly shall flow rivers of living water, and they shall flow into everlasting life." And He spoke of this same water to the woman at the well: "He that shall drink of the water that I shall give him, shall not thirst forever." "If you had asked it of Me," He says, "I would have given it to you." "Sir," said the woman, "give me this water that I may not have to come here and draw." Then Our Lord said: "First go and call your husband [which is self- knowledge], and confess to Me that in your depth you have been no better than a cistern, for all the time you have neglected to drink from these living waters; and then they may be given to you. Also, you have had five husbands (that is to say, your five senses). Alas, you have lived with them, used them for your pleasure, and made yourself unworthy of the living fountain by inordinately clinging to the life of the senses. But now leave them behind, and turn back to Me, and I shall give you welcome."

You will find Our Lord speaking again through Jeremiah in the fourth chapter. It again is a lament, and He says: "I planted you a chosen vineyard, and I expected that you would have produced for Me the best wine of Cyprus, wine of Engaddi." And He speaks of the great labor He spent upon His vineyard: "I have dug it over," he says, "made a hedge round about it, and dug it in a press, and gathered out the stones." Though God spoke thus to His chosen people, He meant it for all men until the end of the world. "You have become bitter to Me, you have yielded sour wine, bitter and acid. And instead of the finest wine and grapes, you have given me wild grapes and barren shoots, and for this I must contend with you. You only return to Me, and I will pour into you living waters and true love."

A great master named Richard [of St. Victor], a scholar of Holy

Scripture, has written of this living water. According to him, love has four degrees. The first degree he calls "wounded love," because the soul is wounded by the rays of God's love so that she may be given the living waters of true love. Then she in her turn wounds God with her love. Of this love Our Lord spoke in the Book of Love: "My Sister, you have wounded my heart with one of your eyes, and with one hair of your neck." The single eye means the eager gazing of mind and heart on God alone, and the single hair is the pure, unalloyed love by which God is said to be wounded.

The second degree is called "captive love." For it is written: "I will draw you with the cords of love."

The third degree is "languishing love." Of this the Bride in the Book of Love says: "I adjure you; O daughters of Jerusalem, if you find my Beloved, that you tell Him that I languish with love."

The fourth degree is "consuming love," of which the Prophet speaks in the One-hundred-eighteenth Psalm: "Deficit—my love is consumed and has fainted, Lord, with longing after Your salvation."

Now let us dwell a little on the first two kinds of love. Concerning "wounded love," we may use a parable. The wounded soul is like a merchant who would charter a ship for the sake of gain. His heart, as it were, is wounded with the desire to carry together all sorts of goods: He gathers his cargo here and there in order to fill up his ship. This is just what the wounded soul does: It gathers into itself all the images, thoughts, and practices it can collect in order to please the Beloved to Whom it has given its heart. And when the ship is fully laden, it launches it and lets out the sails. Our merchant is still master of his ship and is well able to brave the storms. So it is with a person wounded by love. He throws his ship into the storm of the Godhead, steers it gloriously, playing with the wind as is his custom, and finally throws away its oars into the fathomless sea. As the divine effluence rises higher, the sails unfurl more widely, for God now swells them to their utmost capacity, and in doing so He creates further receptivity, and new breadth, thus causing fresh wounds of love.

Now Our Lord cuts the rigging in two and lets the ship run head-on into the storm. Neither rudder nor oar could check her now. Such a man no longer has power over himself, and this is "captive love." Now he fares like a knight who is gravely wounded in battle; his wounds make it still possible to escape, but if he is captured, he is no longer master over himself. Neither thoughts nor actions are now under his control, for he must surrender himself entirely to the Beloved and to love.

Much more could be said of this love. Perhaps we shall continue on some future occasion.

May Eternal Love grant that we may forsake all cisterns and let the waters of pure love be poured into us.

AMEN.

SERMON 19
[ASCENSION II]

Ascendens Christus in altum, captivam duxit captivatatem
Ascending on high, He led captivity captive (Eph 4:8)

The second interpretation of Our Lord's Ascension speaks of five types of activity in which men are held in this world; it also speaks of the means by which the Evil Spirit captures them, and in what way they can regain their freedom.

Our Lord Jesus Christ ascended into Heaven and with Him He led captivity captive. We find five types of captivity in this world to which people are subjected and robbed of their freedom, but when Christ takes us up in His Ascension, He frees us from all our bonds.

The first type of captivity consists in man's dependence on creatures, animate or inanimate, when he loves them without reference to God. This is particularly true of the love of human beings, for who is closer to man than man? The damage that is caused by such inordinate affection cannot be sufficiently stressed. It affects people in two ways: The first are conscious of this evil; they are distressed and fearful and it causes them remorse and self-reproach. This is a wholesome and good sign, because it shows that God has not forsaken them; He summons them day and night, even while they are eating or drinking. If they do not close their ears to the call but listen to it, they will yet be saved.

Others, however, feel quite free in this harmful captivity. They are completely deaf and blind and feel comfortable enough in their self-righteousness. They perform a number of good works, they chant and study pious texts, they observe silence, they render all sorts of services and do a lot of praying, but all this they perform in order to have it both ways. It enables them all the more to use God and the world for their own enjoyment. They impress people with their devoutness, they even shed some pious tears, and on the whole they are pretty content. Such people are in a precarious position indeed, because the devil himself causes this state to keep them in captivity. Nature, too, deceives them, and so they are greatly and dangerously exposed to temptation. It would be better for them not to pray while in this state, far better, for now they only pray against themselves.

The second type of captivity is the lot of those who, after being released from the first—the love of creatures and the world—fall into the captivity of self-love. This love fills them with such complacency that it makes one wonder. No one rebukes them, least of all do they rebuke themselves. Their self-love is so beautifully cloaked, so splendidly projected, that no one could possibly object. Eventually it makes them seek their own in everything: Personal advantage is what they pursue in their pleasures, their consolations, their comfort, and their honor. So totally are they absorbed in themselves that they even make use of God. Alas, what will come to light when the depths of such souls are searched! What appears as sanctity will be found fraudulent throughout. Oh, how hard it will be to help such people with their soft natures and wordly dispositions! How hard it will be to free them from their captivity! When one is confined by nature to such a degree, who can help? Surely none but God. They seem to require so many things, their needs are so extensive and various, and they consider themselves so fragile and sensitive. But when it happens, as it often does, that their possessions are taken from them or threatened, whether it is some convenience or a friend, or another precious thing that lends them comfort, then they immediately reject God with angry words and spiteful actions, speaking untruths openly or by insinuation. Once a person acts in such a way he is dehumanized, no better than a rabid dog or a raging wolf, so pernicious a captivity can self-love be.

The third type of captivity is that of natural reason. This is the downfall of many, because they spoil everything which should be born in the spirit—be it doctrine or truth of whatever kind—by lowering it to the level of their reasoning powers. They give themselves great airs, because whatever it is, they interpret it rationally and hold forth on it, which greatly increases their self-esteem. In that way they neither achieve good works nor develop an interior life. Even the dearest person of Our Lord Jesus Christ, our model, is viewed by them through the eyes of natural reason; if they were but to view it through divine and spiritual eyes, they would see Him in a very different light; it would be as different as the light of a taper and that of the noonday sun, although the difference between natural light and divine light is vastly greater. The natural light is all outward brilliance; it reflects pride, conceit, and delights in the praise of others and in the applause and approval of the world. Its whole tendency is outward, directed toward the dissipation of the senses and the mind. The divine light, on the other hand, if truly present, tends toward inwardness and depth; it makes the soul bend down deeply to the ground, because it feels itself the least, the most insignificant, the weakest and blindest among all creatures; and this is as it should be, for whatever it is that is at its core is surely, wholly of God. Also this light points inward; it seeks the interior ground from which it originated and to which it speeds back with all its might. A man's whole interior activity now tends toward the roots from which he sprang and to which he again wishes to return. This is why we observe such a great difference between those who live the Scriptures and those who merely study them. Those who only study them desire worldly esteem and praise, and they hold those who try to live according to the Evangelical Counsels in low esteem; they think them foolish and perverse, and go so far as to condemn and persecute them with their curses. Those, however, who model their lives after the Gospel consider themselves sinners and show mercy to the others. In the end their fate will differ even more than their life did: life for the one and death for the other. As Saint Paul says: "The letter kills, but the spirit gives life."

And now we come to the fourth captivity, which is that of spiritual sweetness. Many a man has been led astray by it, because he pursued it in an undisciplined way, sunk down in it, and came to a standstill there; it seemed to him a good thing to possess and to abandon himself to with pleasure. But nature will claim its share, and when we think we have grasped God, it is only our own enjoyment we have grasped. Still, there is a way of telling whether God or nature is the source of our joy. If we feel restless and distressed and are troubled as soon as the sweetness begins to fade and diminish, if we are unable to serve God as willingly and as faithfully as before, then we may be sure that it was not really God we served. It is quite possible to enjoy this sweetness for forty years, and then, when it is

71

withdrawn, we could still come to grief. Even if a man should have reached the highest degree of this sweetness and remained in it to the end, it still is up to God's good pleasure whether or not he will be saved. Until the final moment no one is sure of salvation.

The fifth captivity is self-will. By this we mean the will to have one's own way, even in the things of God, even in God Himself. Suppose God were to give Himself to our very will and desires, so much so that we might be rid of all our shortcomings and gain every virtue and perfection; it would indeed be folly to reject such an offer. And yet I can think of something better: Even if I could have my way, with God's consent, I would still say: "No, Lord, not my graces or gifts are what I desire; not my will, Lord, but Yours I shall accept; and should you will that I have nothing, I will surrender for the sake of your will."

To think in such a way, and to renounce self-will with such a disposition, is to possess and receive more than could ever have been gained by having one's own way. Whatever a man may desire to have according to his will, be it God or creatures, it would be infinitely more beneficial to forgo it willingly and humbly and to hold whatever he has, in a spirit of true abandonment, surrendering the will completely to God. For that reason I would prefer a man who was utterly surrendered, with fewer works and accomplishments, to one of dazzling works of virtue whose surrender was imperfect.

While Our Lord still lived with His disciples, they felt such an extraordinary affection for His humanity that it prevented them from attaining to His divinity. Hence he said to them: "It is better for you that I go. For if I go not, the Holy Spirit Who is the Paraclete will not come to you." They still had to wait forty days until He was lifted up to Heaven, taking with Him all their minds and hearts and glorifying them. And then ten days had to pass before the Holy Spirit, the true Comforter, was sent to them. What were days to them are years for us. Their period of waiting was shortened; one day counted as much as a year, because they were destined to be the foundation of the Church.

Until a man has reached his fortieth year, he will never attain lasting peace, never be truly formed into God, try as he may. Up to that time he is occupied by so many things, driven this way and that by his own natural impulses; he is governed by them although he may imagine that he is governed by God. Before the proper time has arrived, he cannot achieve true and perfect peace, nor can he enter into a God-seeing life. After that he shall wait another ten years before the Holy Ghost, the Comforter, the Spirit Who teaches all things, is truly his. Thus the disciples had to wait another ten days in spite of their having been prepared by their lives and by their sufferings; they had forsaken all things and had received the supreme preparation of parting with the One whom they had loved above all, for whose sake they had left everything; even after He had carried their minds and hearts with Him into Heaven, when all their desires, their love, their heart and soul were wholly in Him and with Him in Heaven. After all this delay, after all the sublime instruction, they still had to wait ten days until they received the Holy Spirit. They were assembled together in seclusion and they waited.

And so a man should act when, at the age of forty, he is now in possession of peace, has attained a godly life, and has more or less overcome nature; another ten years will have to go by till he reaches his fiftieth year. Now he may receive the Holy Spirit in the loftiest and most sublime manner, that Holy Spirit Who will teach him all truth. If the soul has reached this point, it will turn into itself to sink down and be immersed and melted into the pure, divine, simple, and innermost core, where the sublime spark of the soul flows back to the source from which it sprang. Wherever this return is freely accomplished, all guilt is wiped away, even if it were the accumulated guilt of mankind since the beginning of the world. From this source all grace and all bliss flow into man's soul. Now he has become divinized, a pillar supporting the world and the Holy Church.

AMEN.

SERMON 21
[ASCENSION IV]

Hic Jesus qui assumptus est a vobis in coelum . . .
This Jesus Who has been taken from you into Heaven . . .
(Acts 1:11)

The fourth Sermon for the Ascension teaches us to seek
peace in the midst of trials, joy in tribulation, and comfort
in bitterness. We are to be God's witnesses on earth, following Him not only in good times but also in sadness and
affliction.

"This is Jesus, Who has been taken from you into Heaven. No
man has ascended into Heaven, but He Who descended
from Heaven," that is Christ, as the Gospel tells us. Beloved, now
that Christ, our Head, has ascended into Heaven, it is fitting to say
that the members should follow Him Who is their Head. It is not for
us to find a lasting habitation in this world; we should follow Him
with love and longing and take the path which He has trodden before
us with so much suffering. "For it was needful for Christ to suffer
thus, and so to enter into His Glory." We are to follow Him, Who
has borne the standard before us. Let every man take up his cross
and follow Him and he will arrive at the place where He is. You
know how a man will follow the ways of the world for empty honors;
how he will forsake his friends, his home, and his family and go out
to war, only to win possessions and worldly esteem. In the same
manner we must follow Christ, our Head, by putting all our trust in
Him Who is our noblest good. There is no member of the body that
is not united to the Head. Any limb which did not receive the constant flow of life from the head would decay, and would have to be
cut off without delay.

Our Lord said to His disciples: "You shall be my witnesses in Judea, in Jerusalem, and Samaria until the end of the World." Jerusalem was a city of peace, but also of tribulation, for there Christ underwent such great suffering and died such a bitter death. In that city we are to be His witnesses, not merely by words, but also in truth and by our actions, by following Him according to our strength.

Many people would gladly be God's witnesses when everything goes according to their wishes. They like to be holy, as long as their devotions are not too much of a burden; they would be happy enough to experience great fervor and profess their faith openly, if only there were no distress, no grief, no drudgery involved. Once, however, they know the terrors and temptations of spiritual darkness, as soon as they no longer experience the emotional comfort of God's closeness, and feel forsaken within and without, they turn back and they are no witnesses at all. All men desire peace and they look for it in all kinds of ways and places. Oh, if they only could free themselves of this illusion, and learn to look for it in tribulation. Only there is born abiding peace, lasting peace that will endure; if you look for it elsewhere, you will fail miserably. You ought to seek joy in sadness, detachment in the midst of disaster, and comfort in bitterness; this is the way to become a true witness of God. Before His death, our Lord always promised peace to His disciples; before and after the Resurrection He did so. And yet they never obtained an outward peace. Nonetheless, they found peace in sorrow, and joy in tribulation. In death they found life, and to be judged, sentenced, and condemned was for them a joyous victory. They were God's witnesses.

I have known people so drenched with sweet consolations that they were felt in every fiber of their being. And yet, when darkness and affliction came upon them, they were left disconsolate, without and within. They did not know which way to turn; they fell behind and it all came to nothing. When we are tossed about by terrible storms which make havoc of our interior balance; when exterior temptations of the world and the flesh and the devil assail us; if then only we could break through and weather such storms, we would arrive at that peace which no one can take from us. Anyone who fails to follow that path will be left behind and never attain this goal. The others, however, will be the true witnesses of Christ.

"You shall be witnesses to me in Judea." Judea signifies "to confess God" or "to praise Him." We are to be God's witnesses by confessing and intending Him in all our actions and endeavors, not only when all goes well, and when we are filled with the warmth of natural enthusiasm. People find it easy enough to confess God at such times. They know and love Him well enough until they are assailed by terrible trials. Then they seem to have forgotten what they had been about, and now that sufferings are upon them, they completely lose their moorings. They are not anchored in God but in their own feelings: a weak foundation indeed, and one built upon shifting sands.

Those, however, who are God's true witnesses are firmly anchored in Him, in love or in suffering, no matter what God may choose to give or take away. They do not set much store by their own methods; if they prove helpful to their spiritual life, well and good. But God, in His loving foresight, often shatters their foundations and thus they frequently find themselves thwarted. If they want to keep vigil, they are obliged to sleep; if they like to fast, they are made to eat; if they would like to keep silence and be at rest, they have to do otherwise. In this way, everything they cleave to crumbles, and they are brought face-to-face with their bare nothingness. Thus they are shown how total is their dependence on God, and they learn to confess Him with a pure and simple faith, with no other support to sustain them. For just as worldly and frivolous people are seduced by the pleasures of their possessions, so these [religious] people take pleasure in their complacency, both in their actions and in their emotions. And thus they are prevented from an absolute surrender to God and from a true poverty of spirit according to God's will.

Judea also stands for "praising God." If we could only learn to praise God in everything—in our thoughts and works and in all events, whether they turn out to our advantage or not. Then we should have discovered the right way. And furthermore, if we could refer everything back to God, with heartfelt gratitude, then we should be true and steadfast witnesses indeed. Beloved, return all things to the ground of Being from which they originated, never come to a standstill at created things, but unite yourselves with them to the uncreated Source. Within its depth is born true praise of God, and there it grows and blooms and bears fruit. Blossom and fruit become one, and we discover God in God and light in light. Carry back, then, all cares and concerns of body and soul, carry them back to God, and offer them to Him and yourself with them.

Christ also said: "You shall be witnesses in Samaria." Samaria means "union with God." Surely the closest and most direct way of bearing witness is to be truly united with Him. In this way the soul takes flight away from itself and from all creatures, for in the simple unity of the Divine Godhead it sheds all multiplicity. It is now exalted above itself. The highest faculties of the soul are raised up into Heaven where God in his Majesty dwells in Unity. There the soul experiences beatitude and inexpressible joy in God. Even the lower faculties are raised up as far as this is possible. In such a state a man can lose himself entirely in God. Nothing remains for him but to praise Him for all the loving and glorious gifts He has bestowed upon him, for now he understands that they are all God's and he does not attribute them to himself.

Beyond this, he is led into another Heaven which is the divine Essence itself, where the [human] spirit loses itself so completely that no trace of the self remains. What happens to him there, what he experiences and enjoys, no man can ever tell or conceive or understand. Indeed, how could the mind ever grasp such a thing? Even the spirit of man cannot comprehend it, for so submerged is it now into the divine ground that it knows nothing, feels nothing, understands nothing but God alone in His simple, pure, undisguised Unity. Now the human spirit is enabled to glance back and examine its humblest acts, whether perhaps there is anything that has escaped its attention; anything which is in need of perfecting, or required to be carried out in another way. And thus man is truly suspended between Heaven and earth: With his higher faculties he is exalted above himself and above all things and dwells in God. With his lower faculties he is brought low, into the depths of his humility, as if he were a beginner in the spiritual life. He is not above undertaking the simplest devotions that he performed when he was a novice. He despises nothing, no matter how insignificant, and finds peace in all that he does. Thus he has become a true witness of Our Lord bearing witness that it is He Who came down from Heaven and again ascended into Heaven, indeed above all the heavens.

Anyone who wishes to reach this summit must be united to Him, in Him, with Him, and through Him. My Beloved! Whoever followed this path would make his journey in safety, without fear of losing his way. He would not be bothered by scruples or by any such questions that arise from an unstable mind and which waste so much time.

May the eternal God help us to attain this state.

AMEN.

SERMON 23
[SUNDAY AFTER ASCENSION]

Estote prudentes et vigilate in orationibus
Be prudent therefore, and watch in prayers (1 Pt 4:9)

This Sermon for the Sunday after Ascension takes its text
from the first Epistle of Saint Peter. It speaks of true detachment and self-denial, of inwardness and solitude as a
means of preparing for the reception of the Holy Spirit.

Holy Church is now celebrating the sending of the Holy Spirit,
who was received by the disciples in a special interior way. It
had to happen in this way because they stood at the beginning. A
new order had to be inaugurated, and therefore this particular way
of reception was necessary for the sake of those who came after them.
The longer the disciples lived, the stronger their experience became,
increasing hour by hour.

In the same way every friend of God should celebrate this very
sweet feast every hour and every day. We should always be receiving
the Holy Spirit. He comes to us according to our preparedness, and
the more receptive we are, the more perfectly He will be received.
This visible coming, which was the share of the disciples on the day
of Pentecost, happens in a spiritual way at all times to those who are
perfectly prepared. Thus He comes to each of us in a special way,
with new and special graces all our life long, provided that we turn
toward Him and are ready for His Coming.

Now along comes Saint Peter to instruct us clearly and beyond
a doubt what we have to do to prepare for the Holy Spirit. "*Estote
prudentes*," he says. This does not exactly mean "be wise." A better
reading would be "act with discernment," the discernment one ac-
quires when one has practiced a thing often and well and now knows

it thoroughly. This is what Saint Peter has in mind when he advises us to select in every instance what is the best means of accomplishing our aims in the light of reason, so that we know what we are about. In this case it is detachment and surrender to God, inwardness and spiritual solitude, which prepare for the Coming of the Sweet Holy Spirit. This is the disposition which enables us to receive Him in a lofty and unimpeded way. Whoever is in possession of these means and grows in them is indeed capable in the highest degree to receive Him.

What, then, does true detachment, the first of the four requisites, really mean? It means that we must turn away and withdraw from all that is not God pure and simple; that we reflect in the light of reason on our words and thoughts and deeds in an understanding spirit to see if there is perhaps anything that is not oriented toward God as its sole and supreme Good. Let us rid ourselves of anything that is not directed toward Him. This applies not only to those who wish to lead a spiritual life, but to all good men. How many good persons do we come across who perform great good works and yet are ignorant of the interior life! They, too, are bound to consider what interposes itself between them and God, so that they may abandon and completely avoid it. This degree of detachment is imperative if one wishes to receive the Holy Spirit and His gifts. It is essential to turn totally to God and away from all that is not God.

This detachment and expectation of the Holy Spirit manifests itself differently in different people. Some receive the Holy Spirit by way of their senses, through sensible images. Others receive Him in a loftier manner, by way of their higher powers, by that reason which is so far superior to the senses. The third group receives Him beyond mode or manner, within that hidden abyss, that secret realm, that blissful ground where the noble image of the Blessed Trinity dwells. A more precious place the soul does not possess.

Oh, with what sweet joy does the Holy Spirit make His abode there! Here His gifts are received in a supreme way and in a divine fashion. Each time we gaze upon this ground by the light of reason and turn to God there comes about a renewed union and an infusion of the Holy Spirit at every moment. And we receive new gifts and graces as often as we turn inward, examining the purity of our intentions with discernment and detachment. Is there perhaps anything in our conduct that is not purely directed toward God? If there is, let high reason correct and govern it. This light is to illuminate the natural virtues, such as humility, gentleness, goodness, mercy, silence, and the like, to see whether they are born of God or not.

This light is to illuminate the moral virtues as well, such as prudence, justice, fortitude, and temperance. They are called chief or cardinal virtues, and the light of reason must examine them too as to purity of intention so that the divine order may reign in them and they may be practiced in God and through Him. When the Holy Spirit finds that we have done our part, He comes with His light, which outshines all natural light and infuses supernatural virtues such as faith, hope, and charity, and the accompanying graces. In this manner, detachment brings about true nobility. But unless it is truly illuminated, it comes to nothing; for it frequently appears that we intended God, and yet we discover that this was not the case at all.

Still, we should note at this point that, although our desires were centered on God, we can at times be afflicted with anxiety and sadness, fearing that it was not God at all we meant and that now all is lost. Sometimes that fear may be caused by a natural tendency toward melancholy, by the air or climate, or even by the devil. All this we should overcome by gentle patience.

There are people who would overcome these difficulties by violence, by one single stroke. They only do themselves harm by causing such tumult. Others will run and consult the learned or the friends of God, but no one can give much help, and their confusion only increases. The best thing to do when such a storm comes upon the soul is to act like people who have been caught in a cloudburst; they take shelter under a roof and await the end of the storm. This is what we should do when we are certain that it is God alone we are seeking. When the trouble arises, we should ignore it till we have found peace, waiting in submission and patient surrender for God in our anguish. Who knows where and when and by what means God will choose to come and bestow His gifts? It is a hundred times better to stand patiently under the shelter of the divine will than to aspire toward high virtue with its full-blown emotional satisfactions which we love so dearly. For in this state there can be no clinging to our selfhood, as happens so easily when we feel spiritual fervor and comfort. There, nature claims its own, seizes God's gifts, and takes pleasure in them. This causes a stain upon the soul, for God's gifts are not God. Our joy should be God alone and not His gifts. Now, our nature is so acquisitive and so selfish that it creeps in everywhere, claiming what does not rightfully belong to it. Thus it spoils and sullies God's gifts and impedes His noble work. So permeated is our nature with the poison of Original Sin that it seeks its own in everything. Saint Thomas says that on account of this we love ourselves more than God or His Angels or anything else God has created. Not that God made our nature like this; it has become corrupted and disfigured by turning away from Him.

So deeply rooted is this poison in the inmost recesses of the soul that all the experts in the world cannot trace all its ramifications, nor will they ever succeed in rooting it out. This corrupt tendency very often comes to light when one thinks one has found God. There one most frequently comes upon this poisonous self-seeking, for man has his own interest at heart in all that he does. Saint Paul showed himself a true prophet when he said that in the last days men shall be great lovers of themselves. All the world over we observe, alas, how men will rob one another of their rights by injustice, fraud, and violence; how they seek confessors after their own hearts; and how they will make use of strange texts from pagan authors to interpret Scripture their own way. I mention all this by way of illustrations drawn from external things. The same is true to a far greater extent in spiritual matters, for there a true, pure treasure is at stake. It is a small matter to lose a castle and lands, or gold and silver, compared to the possessiveness inside, be it in spiritual or natural things, toward the practice of virtue or even toward God Himself. Corrupt nature constantly makes its inroads, and before we are aware of it everything is flooded with disordered self-love.

For this reason our dear Lord added to Saint Peter's injunction to be prudent another counsel: He tells us to be wise as serpents. Note how the eternal Son of God, the Wisdom of the Father, always hid the ineffable brilliance of His wisdom in simple every-day parables. As He was humble throughout, so was His teaching always humble and simple. Listen now in what the prudence of a serpent consists. When the serpent finds that it becomes old and shriveled and decaying, it looks for a place where there are two stones close together, and it drags itself through the narrow space between them. In this way the old skin is shed, and underneath another is newly formed. That is just what we ought to do with our old skin, that is, whatever is ours by nature, however grand and good it may seem. It certainly has grown old and full of defects and must be drawn through two stones lying very close together.

And what are these two stones? One is the eternal Godhead which is the Truth; the other is the adorable humanity of Christ which is the true Way. Between these two stones a man must draw his whole life and being, in case there is still something of the old man that may cling to his virtues, whether natural or moral. Of this the Church will soon be singing: "*Sine tuo numine, nihil est in lumine, nihil est innoxium*"—"Without your divinity nothing is in the light, nothing is innocent." Therefore examine carefully whatever virtues you may possess, however subtle and noble they may be. If they are grounded merely in nature, they cause spiritual ulcers, and the more cleverly you practice them, the swifter will be the damage. If, on the other hand, they are moral virtues and lofty aspirations, they, too, can cause spiritual stains and signs of aging. Unless they are sharpened by the stone which is Christ, and renewed by inward desire and heartfelt prayers; unless they are dipped into God and reborn and newly made, they are of no avail and will not be pleasing in God's sight.

This is the stone, so worthy of our love, of which Saint Paul says that it is the foundation of the whole building and it is also the cornerstone to which the Lord Himself refers. If you are not sharpened thoroughly by this stone, all Solomon's wisdom and all Solomon's strength will be of no avail.

Immerse yourself in the poverty of Christ, in His chastity, in His obedience. Let Him do away with your frailties, let Him free you of all merely natural virtue, so that you may receive in Him the seven gifts of the Holy Spirit together with the three theological virtues of faith, hope, and charity and all perfection, truth, peace, and joy in the Holy Spirit. From Him arises detachment, patience, and a spirit of equanimity in which one accepts all things as coming from God.

Whatever God ordains or allows in our regard, happiness or misfortune, pleasure or pain, it all contributes toward our eternal bliss; for everything that comes to us has been foreseen by God from all eternity. It has always existed in His mind, where it was decreed that things should happen in this manner and not in another. Thus we should be at peace about it all. This peace under all circumstances is acquired only by true detachment and inwardness. Whoever wishes to attain it must learn it in this way and seek it in a spirit of inward recollection, for thus only will it be established and take root.

All that I have preached to you in this sermon is addressed to the spiritual man; let him bear the counsels continually in mind, and let him regulate his conduct accordingly. It will be quite possible for him to do so when the tranquillity of his soul is rooted and grounded in God; when his desire is directed wholly toward God. In this light he will know and understand all virtues for what they are, sloughing them off by the help of Christ. This is the way of all those who are born anew and are strengthened interiorly in true detachment. The more this interior process increases, the more richly the Holy Spirit is given, the more gloriously He is received.

As for the rest of Saint Peter's text, we shall have something to say about it in the next sermon.

God grant that we may all seek Him in a true spirit of detachment, with a pure and inward aspiration. May God, our Beloved, be Himself our help in this.

AMEN.

SERMON 24
[MONDAY BEFORE PENTECOST]

Estote prudentes et vigilate in orationibus
Live wisely, and keep your senses awake to greet the
hours of prayer (1 Pt 4:8)

A second interpretation of this passage from the Epistle of
Saint Peter urges us to direct all our actions toward God
and to eradicate, turn over, and cut down all that is not
His, just as a farmer prunes his trees, weeds his garden,
and reploughs his ground when March is near.

Saint Peter said in his letter: "Live wisely, and keep your senses
awake to greet the hours of prayer." And since we are now approaching the lovely feast of the Holy Spirit, we should prepare ourselves with all our strength to receive Him with a heart abounding
in holy desire. As we said yesterday, we must search, in a spirit of
discernment, whether there is perhaps anything in our actions and
in our lives that is not of God. We mentioned that this preparation
falls into four parts: detachment, abandonment, inwardness, and
single-mindedness. Furthermore it is necessary that the outer man
be at peace and well versed in the natural virtues, the lower faculties
governed by the moral virtues, after which the Holy Spirit will
adorn the higher faculties with infused virtues. All this must, of
course, be ordered and directed by true discernment and applied to
our lives by the light of reason. Let everyone examine, first, whether
his life is wholly directed toward God, and should he discover anything in his actions that is not, let him correct it.

In all this we should proceed precisely like a farmer who in
March sets out to prepare his ground; when he sees the sun climbing
higher, he trims and prunes his trees, he pulls up the weeds, and

turns over the ground, digging diligently. In the same manner we should work deeply into our ground, examine it, and turn it over thoroughly. Now it is time to prune the trees—our exterior senses and faculties—and see that the weeds be pulled out completely. We ought to begin by clipping away the seven Deadly Sins thoroughly and boldly. We should get rid of all pride in its exterior and interior form; do away with avarice, anger, hatred, and envy, and all impurity and covetousness in body, heart, senses, and mind. This applies to the natural as well as to the spiritual level. We must also look for false and hidden motives and any tendency toward self-indulgence. All this should be cut off and eradicated entirely.

At this point, however, the soil is still dry and hard. Though the sun is beginning to ascend, its rays have not yet penetrated the wintry earth. Still, it is climbing higher now, swiftly, and the summer is rapidly approaching. Now it is time for the divine sun to shine upon the well-prepared ground. As soon as the outer man has prepared his lower and higher faculties, the whole of him becomes receptive, and the tender, divine sun begins to send its bright rays into his noble ground; and now a joyous summer commences, a downright may-blossoming is about to unfold. The gracious, eternal God permits the spirit to green and bloom and bring forth the most marvelous fruit, surpassing anything a tongue can express and a heart can conceive. Such is the rapture that arises within the spirit.

As soon as the Holy Spirit can come with His presence and freely flood the depth of the soul with His wondrous radiance and divine light, then He, who is rightly called the Comforter, is able to exercise His sweet comfort there—oh, what a blissful rapture is now to occur! There is holiday feasting everywhere, and the kitchen abounds in sweet fragrances of rich and rare dishes. What savory and delicious fare is being prepared there, and how it draws us by its scent! May has arrived and stands in full bloom. These aromatic sweets reach far out into poor human nature, which now has a fair share in these joys. The ecstasy which the Holy Spirit so richly and generously bestows as a gift upon the well-prepared soul, oh, could one savor just a single drop, it would exceed and extinguish any taste for all the sweetness that created things can offer in any way known or imagined.

Now, as soon as some people discover and experience this rare comfort, they would like to immerse themselves and fall asleep in it, rest forever in its bliss, just as Saint Peter, tasting one drop of this joy, wished to build three tents and remain there forever. But this was not Our Lord's wish; for the goal to which he would guide and lead him was still far off. And as it was with Saint Peter, who exclaimed, "It is good for us to be here," so it is with us: As soon as we become aware of this bliss, we believe ourselves in possession of the entire sun, and we would like to bask in its radiance and stretch out under its warmth. Those who act thus will always remain in the same place; nothing will come of them, they have missed the point.

Others, again, fall into a different trap by wishing to find a false freedom in this sweetness. In this state of emotional joy, nature cleverly turns back upon itself and takes possession; and this is what human nature is most inclined to do, it likes to rely upon emotions. The effect is as bad as with some people who take too many medicines; as soon as nature grows accustomed to them, it becomes dependent, relents, turns lazy, and thinks that it has a good crutch there, and would not work as hard as it would otherwise. If, however, it is left without any assurance of such help, it becomes active again and helps itself. Just observe, Beloved, how sly and treacherous this nature of ours is, and how it invariably seeks its own comfort and convenience. And this is true to a much higher degree in spiritual matters. For, as soon as a man experiences this pleasure and feels this extraordinary well-being, he thinks he can rely upon it. He leans on it and does not work with the same zeal and fidelity as before. He becomes self-indulgent and pampered, imagining that he cannot suffer and work as he used to, and must keep himself in a state of repose. As soon as the devil sees a man in such a condition, he invests it with a false sweetness in order to keep him in his state of treacherous tranquillity.

How, then, should we conduct ourselves in such a case? Shun this sweetness and reject it? Certainly not. It is with immense gratitude that we should receive it, and then humbly offer it back to God, giving Him great thanks and praise and confessing our own unworthiness. We should conduct ourselves like a young man who sets out on a journey: He is poor, hungry, and thirsty and still has a long stretch of road ahead of him. "If I only walk four more miles," he says to himself, "I will get a square meal and then I shall be satisfied and refreshed." At this thought his cheerfulness and strength return, and he can happily walk another ten miles. That is precisely the way in which we should act when God strengthens and feeds us with sweet comfort and spiritual joys; everything should increase: our love, our gratitude, our praise, our intention to live according to His will. We should stretch toward God in sweet longing and ardent love and be so consumed in this service that God would rightfully multiply His gifts of comfort and spiritual delectation.

This could also be compared to a man who wished to see the Pope to make him a gift of one single florin and the Pope came out to meet him and gave him a hundred thousand pounds of gold in return, and he would repeat this over and over again, each time the man offered a florin; this is the way God deals with us when we turn to Him with gratitude, making an offering of ourselves with love and thankfulness. Each time, God hastens toward us with more and more gifts and graces, more sweet comfort at every single moment. In this manner [the gift of] spiritual consolation turns into a help, and a means to God and thus to a higher good. We should avail ourselves of such comfort, but not for its own sake, just as a man who travels in a carriage enjoys it not for its own sake but for its usefulness. So, too, it is with God's gifts: They are to be used, but God alone is to be enjoyed.

Saint Peter tells us to beware of this harm, and he admonishes us to live wisely, and to keep our senses awake; he warns us not to fall asleep cradled by this comfort, for a sleeping man is as it were half dead and unable to act on his own accord. We should keep our senses awake and be brave and sober. A sober person performs his work cheerfully, courageously, and intelligently. That is why Saint Peter says: "Brethren, be sober and watchful; the devil who is your adversary goes about roaring like a lion, to find his prey, but you, grounded in faith, must face him boldly." Beloved! Be not drowsy and indolent, and do not persevere in anything that is not entirely of God. Glance watchfully around you and, guided by your reason, attend to yourselves and to God within you in loving desire.

For not even the loving disciples of Our Lord himself were granted to remain in the joy of His Presence, should they become partakers of the Holy Spirit. "If I should not go from you," said the Lord, "the Spirit, the Comforter, cannot come to you!" So filled were the holy disciples, inwardly and outwardly, by the joyful presence of Our Lord Jesus Christ, so saturated were their hearts, souls, minds, and faculties, that every trace of the attachment had to be taken from them, to make room for the true, spiritual, interior consolation. This plenitude of exterior comfort had to leave them, however bitter it might have seemed at the time, if they were ever to progress and not remain on the lowest level, that of the senses. Once, however, man transcends the senses, he enters the realm of the higher faculties, those of the intellect, and here this comfort is received in a manner more lofty and sublime; from here we attain the interior ground, the sanctuary of the spirit, and this is the proper dwelling-place of such joy; here it is received in essence and in reality; here, in all sobriety, we partake of the fullness of life.

Now Saint Peter says: "Be watchful in prayer, for the adversary goes about like a roaring lion." What kind of prayer does Saint Peter have in mind? Is it the prayer of the mouth, practiced by people who reel off the Psalter that way? No, that is not what he meant. He rather meant the prayer which Our Lord called true prayer, when He called true worshipers those who pray in spirit and in truth. The saints and spiritual masters tell us that prayer is an ascent of the mind to God; reading and vocal prayer can occasionally help us to achieve this, and to that extent they may be useful. Just as my cloak and my clothes are not me and yet serve me, so also vocal prayer serves and leads occasionally to true prayer, although it falls short of being that by itself. For true prayer is a direct raising of the mind and heart to God, without intermediary. This and nothing else is the essence of prayer.

This loving ascent to God, in profound longing and humble surrender, that one is true prayer; nevertheless, the clergy, religious, and those who receive benefices are bound to the recitation of the canonical hours and to vocal prayer; but no external prayer is as devout and as deserving of our love as is the sacred Our Father. The greatest of all the masters taught it to us and said it Himself. More than any other, it leads to essential prayer; indeed it is a heavenly prayer. This true prayer is said and contemplated in Heaven without ceasing: It is a genuine ascent to God, a lifting of the spirit upward, so that God may in reality enter the purest, most inward, noblest part of the soul—its deepest ground—where alone there is undifferentiated unity.

In regard to this Saint Augustine says that the soul has a hidden abyss, untouched by time and space, which is far superior to anything that gives life and movement to the body. Into this noble and wondrous ground, this secret realm, there descends that bliss of which we have spoken. Here the soul has its eternal abode. Here a man becomes so still and essential, so single-minded and withdrawn, so raised up in purity, and more and more removed from all things, for God Himself is present in this noble realm, and works and reigns and dwells therein. This state of the soul cannot be compared to what it has been before, for now it is granted to share in the divine life itself. The spirit meets wholly with God and enflames itself in all things, and is drawn into the hot fire of love, which is God in essence and in nature.

And from this height such men descend again into all the needs of Christendom, and in holy prayer and desire address themselves to everything God wills to be prayed for. They pray for their friends, for sinners, for the souls in purgatory; their charity embraces every man's need in holy Christendom. Not that they petition God for each person's selfish desires; their prayer is simple and wise. Just as I see you all sitting before me at once glance, so they draw all into their embrace in this same abyss, in this fire of love, as in a divine contemplation. Then they turn their gaze back to this loving abyss, to this fire of love, and there they rest; and after plunging into it, they descend to all who are in want until they return to the loving, dark, silent rest of the abyss.

Thus they go in and out, and yet remain at all times within, in the sweet, silent ground in which they have their substance and life, in which they move and have their being. Wherever one finds such men, one finds nothing but divine life. Their conduct, their actions, their whole manner of life is divinized. They are noble souls, and the whole of Christendom draws profit from them. To all they give sustenance, to God glory, and to mankind consolation. They dwell in God, and God in them. Wherever they are they should be praised.

May God grant that we, too, may have a share in this.

AMEN.

SERMON 26

[PENTECOST II]

Repleti sunt omnes Spiritu Sancto
And they were all filled with the Holy Spirit (Acts 2:4)

The second interpretation of the sublime event of Pentecost teaches how to bring ourselves to a focus and to shut out external matters, so that we may prepare a dwelling-place for the Holy Spirit Who makes us receptive to His divine operation within us.

"They were all filled with the Holy Spirit and they began to speak of the wonderful works of God." This is the marvelous day on which the Holy Spirit descended in the form of fiery tongues upon the disciples and upon those who were united with them. This is the day on which the priceless treasure, lost in Paradise through the evil counsel of Satan and human weakness, has been returned. It is the day on which it has been restored to us.

Even the outward circumstances of the event fill us with wonder; but the spiritual reality hidden and contained with it exceeds everything that could be known, conceived, or expressed by any creature. It is past all telling. So incomprehensible is the Holy Spirit in His greatness, so infinite in His loving richness, that all His greatness and infinity eludes any image our human reason could form. Heaven and earth and all they contain are as nothing in comparison. Compared to Him, all creatures together are as small as the tiniest particle beside the whole world. All created beings in their entirety are a thousand times less than the least that may be said of the Holy Spirit. If, therefore, He should be fitly received, it is He who must prepare the place, create the receptiveness in the soul, and also dwell there to receive Himself. It is the ineffable abyss of God that must be His dwelling and the place where He is received, not that of creatures.

"And the whole house was filled." God fulfills wholly. Wherever He enters, He fills the entire capacity of the soul completely, every nook and corner.

The disciples were all filled with the Holy Spirit. First, we must observe what were the circumstances when the disciples were filled with the Holy Spirit, for these should be the same for all of us. They were gathered there, gathered within themselves, and they were sitting still when the Holy Spirit was sent to them. This Holy Spirit, so rich in love, will be sent to each of us as often and as much as we withdraw ourselves from creatures and turn wholly to God. The very instant we do this, the Holy Spirit comes at once with all His gifts, flooding the recesses of the soul down to its very ground. On the other hand, the moment a man turns willfully away from God to creatures, whether it be to himself or to any created thing whatever, the Holy Spirit immediately flees and leaves the soul, taking with Him all the treasures and riches. Wherever such a man now turns without God and outside of God—it is his own self he is seeking.

The house where the disciples were gathered was completely filled. In one sense this house signifies Holy Church, which is indeed God's dwelling-place. In another sense it signifies each man in whom the Holy Spirit dwells. Now, just as there are many dwellings and rooms in one house, so in one man there are many faculties, senses, and activities; and in all these He enters in a special way. When He comes, He urges, impels, and straightens man by His influence and illumination. However, these operations are not perceived by all people in the same manner; for in reality He dwells in the souls of all the just. Yet, if we wish to feel His action, if we desire to savor His presence, then we must bring ourselves to a focus, shut out external matters, and allow the Holy Spirit to unfold within us in stillness and repose. In this manner we first and foremost become aware of Him and so He reveals Himself to us. Our awareness will increase in proportion to our consent. And hour by hour He will reveal Himself more clearly, although He has been given to man from the very beginning.

"The disciples were shut in for fear of the Jews." Dear Lord! How much more necessary is it now for men to flee and shut themselves in from the hateful "Jews" who are surrounding them everywhere? At every corner and in every house they are lurking. Beloved, beware of these dangerous "Jews" who want to deprive you of God and the joy you have in Him, and of that sweet dawning of the Holy Spirit and of His divine comfort. Your need for caution is a thousand times greater than that of the disciples; for the Jews could only take their mortal lives, whereas you may be robbed of God, your souls, and eternal life. Flee from these "Jews," shut yourselves in, and give up your harmful excursions. Shun such occasions and be careful of the company you keep, avoid idle words and works, whatever they may be. Beware of these "Jews" who are peering in at your windows. Beware! They are dangerously close. Otherwise you will drive away the Holy Spirit and lose Him altogether. "Sir," some of you might say, "my confessor said it would not hurt me; after all I mean no harm. I must have some pleasure and diversion." Dear Lord! How can it happen that you fail to desire and delight in the sweet and tender divine good which is eternal and infinitely rich in love? How can you find pleasure and satisfaction, joy and peace in miserable creatures who are out to destroy you? How can it be that you drive away that pure and sublime treasure which created you, the Holy Spirit Who is indeed called the Comforter? And all this is supposed to do no harm! Oh, what a shameful pity! On the other hand, my Beloved, do not shun those wise and blessed men who desire nothing but God and divine things and whose ground is filled with a true longing for God. Even when they venture out into the world, they remain within and at home. Wherever they may turn, they are filled with the Holy Spirit and His peace.

"The disciples were gathered together." Here we are taught to gather up all our faculties, interior and exterior, so that the Holy Spirit may find room to work in us, for wherever He finds a dwelling He works wondrous things. Furthermore, "the disciples were seated when the Holy Spirit descended upon them." So you, too, must have your seat in the truth and assign all created things, joys and sorrows, willing and surrendering, their seat in God's will. This counsel is binding to all who wish to lead a spiritual life. For what is meant by spirituality except to be one with God's will, in harmony and union with Him? Indeed it is an obligation for all Christians who wish to be saved not to will anything contrary to God's will. And yet it is sometimes asked whether religious are obliged to be perfect. "They are obliged," Saint Thomas says, "to live and strive for perfection."

Note that the Holy Spirit, when He enters the soul, imparts seven gifts through which He effects seven works. Three of them prepare man for higher perfection, the remaining four perfect him. They lead the soul, inwardly and without, to the highest, purest, and most lofty stage of true perfection.

The first gift, the fear of God, is a safe and trustworthy beginning, a path we take to reach the highest possible stage. This gift is a mighty wall, secure and strong. It protects us from all shortcomings and obstacles that might ensnare us. In extreme danger of sin, this holy fear bids us to flee, just as a wild animal or bird will shun and swiftly flee from those who would catch or grasp it. Just as God has given this instinct to nature, so the Holy Spirit has imparted this beautiful fear to His own in order that they may be protected from all hindrances that might separate them from Him. Due to the perfection of this holy fear it is able to shield us from the world, from the devil, from ourselves, and all the ways and works by which we might lose spiritual repose and that interior peace which is the place where God truly dwells. We should flee the source of such danger, for our mutable nature is incapable of keeping the balance between God and the world for long. We either surrender to God completely or we do without Him, with the result that we fall into grave and mortal sin, whether we wish it or not. The fear of God teaches us how to avoid such pitfalls, for, as the Prophet says, it is the beginning of wisdom.

After the gift of fear comes that of piety, a gentle and tender gift which lifts us to a higher degree of receptiveness. It frees us from all inordinate sadness and anxiety which may have been caused by holy fear and might have left us in a state of depression. This gift raises us up and brings about a heavenly ease, inward and without, in all circumstances. It takes away dejection, bitterness, and all hardness of heart. It makes us gently disposed toward our neighbor in speech and action; peaceable, loving, and considerate in our conduct toward all. That disposition, first made possible by the fear of God, shields us from impetuosity, which banishes and thrusts out the Holy Spirit.

Next comes the third gift, which carries the soul still higher. Thus the Holy Spirit always leads us from one gift to the other in such a way that each one opens up paths that run closer to perfection than did the previous one. The third gift is that of knowledge. It enables us to listen inwardly to the promptings and warnings of the

Holy Spirit; for, as Our Lord said: "When He shall come, He will teach you all things," that is, all things needful to us. They may be warnings such as "Be on your guard, for the result may be evil; don't say this, don't do that, don't go there." Or again He may counsel: "Conduct yourself in such a way, act now, and be patient in endurance." He wishes to lead our spirit to the very heights—so noble is it—beyond the body, into a spiritual realm. He desires the body to retain its dignity, being practiced in virtue, in trials and rejections patiently borne. God wills that both spirit and body should hold their proper place, so that they may be reunited in a dignity a thousand times higher, devoid of all fear.

Those who are faithful to this gift of knowledge are led to the fourth gift, divine fortitude. It is indeed a noble gift. With it the Holy Spirit elevates us high above human ways, high above all weakness and fear. By this gift the holy martyrs were strengthened to face death joyfully for the sake of God. It is the gift which makes man so high-minded that he would gladly do the works of all; to suffer all things, as Saint Paul said: "I can do all things in Him who strengthens me." Empowered by it, he fears neither fire nor water, neither death nor any other thing. Such a man can say with Saint Paul: "Neither hunger nor thirst nor principalities can separate me from the love of God." By this gift, man becomes so strong that not only would he never commit a mortal sin, but he would die rather than anger God by a venial sin, deliberately or with forethought. We are told by the saints that we ought indeed to prefer death in such a case, but this is a matter I will not take up now. There is no doubt, however, that we ought to die rather than commit a mortal sin against God, with willful knowledge and consent. By virtue of this gift man can accomplish marvelous things.

Now you should know that, when the Holy Spirit comes into the soul, He always brings great love, light, joy, and comfort. For He is called and indeed is the Comforter. When an imprudent person becomes aware of this, he falls upon it with delight and is greatly gratified. But since it is the delight he loves, he incurs the loss of the real good. A wise person treats such gifts in a different manner. He returns to the source and presses on beyond all the graces and gifts till he reaches a blessed and purified love. He does not look this way and that but fixes his glance unswervingly on God.

Now comes the fifth gift, which is counsel. And in what great need we are of it! For at this point God will remove all His previous favors and will leave us to our own resources in order to see, and allow us to see, how we bear ourselves in such a trial. God now lets us sink to the very depth, so that no knowledge of Him remains, no grace, no comfort, nor anything that we or any good person may have ever gained. All this is now totally hidden and removed. In such a state the gift of counsel is sorely needed, in order that we may conduct ourselves in the way God wishes. With its help we learn abandonment, death to self, and surrender to the awesome and secret judgments of God which now painfully deprive us of that sublime and pure good in which we had found our salvation, our joy and comfort.

The soul thus stripped of itself is truly and completely surrendered to God. So deeply has it sunk into the divine will that, if God so wished, it would remain not a week or a month, but a thousand years or forever in this state of poverty and nakedness. Even if it were God's wish that the soul suffer the eternal pains of hell, it would still be totally surrendered. Beloved, this would be true abandonment. Compared to this, it would be a small matter to lose a thousand worlds. So would be the offering of their lives that the saints made with a lightsome heart, gladly and joyously, for they possessed God's powerful comfort within. And yet this was nothing compared to the desolation which is the loss of God experienced by the soul undergoing the trial of being deprived of Him. That anguish surpasses all others.

And then, in addition to this, the temptations and miseries which had been overcome earlier now assail the soul with renewed force, with a force far greater than when it was still struggling against them. Now is the time to let oneself sink into God's arms. For when a person is left to himself, he never remains within. He turns this way and that and is scattered all over the lot. But now he must suffer it all and surrender himself to the very depth. Why, do you suppose, was Saint Peter told to forgive seventy times seven times? Because a human being left to himself is so very weak. Not only seventy times seven is he forgiven, but a thousand, indeed countless times, by day and by night. He is forgiven as often as he turns to God and acknowledges his faith. It is a noble and good thing to confess one's weakness and then always to return to God. In this as in everything else we must follow the counsel to renounce everything, to overcome everything, and to return to the source, the ground which is God's will.

Beloved, with the aid of the first three gifts one can be a good and holy person, but with the last gift one becomes spiritualized and utterly pleasing to God. By this surrender the soul truly sets foot into eternal life. After such a trial it will never know another—neither hell, nor suffering, nor being forsaken by God. It is impossible that God would ever forsake such a soul any more than He would forsake Himself: for the soul has totally surrendered to the One and to the Source. Even if all the anguish and suffering of the entire world fall upon it, the soul would not heed it, nor would it be harmed by it. A sheer joy it would be to these souls, for all things are their realm, and there they move and have their being. They only have to draw after them the other foot that is still in time, and immediately they are in eternal life, which for them had begun here below and shall last forever.

Now we approach the last two gifts, understanding and the wisdom which is a taste of God. These two gifts lead the soul right into the depth, beyond all human ways into the divine abyss where God knows Himself and understands Himself and delights in his own Being.

In this abyss the soul loses itself so deeply, so unfathomably, that it becomes forgetful of its own being, unaware of word or concept, feeling or perception, knowledge or love. There is but the pure simplicity of God, an unfathomable abyss, a being, a spirit. Now God grants the soul by grace that which He is by nature, uniting it with His nameless, unchartered, wayless Being. Here everything that is done in the soul God Himself performs: acting, knowing, loving, praising, enjoying. And the soul lets it be, in a divine passivity. To speak of the soul and how it fares is as impossible as to conceive or express the divine Essence itself, for it is too lofty for the created intellects of both man and Angel, be it by nature or by grace. To this the Holy Spirit leads all those who prepare a dwelling for Him so that He may fulfill those who allow Him to be their host and follow Him. Beloved, how glad, how exceedingly glad we should be to forsake all things and to follow this blessed Spirit Who is given to us today and always, and Who will be given every day and every hour to those who are ready to receive Him. May God grant that we may receive Him in so noble a manner.

AMEN.

SERMON 27

[PENTECOST III]

Dixit Jesus discipulis suis: "Qui non intrat per ostium . . .
Jesus spoke to his disciples: "He that enters not by the
door into the sheepfold . . ." (Jn 10:1)

> The third commentary on the Feast of Pentecost tells us
> that the sheep must enter the sheepfold by the door; this
> signifies that we should be truly God-oriented and let noth-
> ing stand in the way. It also reminds us not to attribute
> anything in the spiritual life to our own rational powers,
> and not to condemn our neighbor.

One day Our Lord Jesus Christ said to His disciples: "Believe me
when I tell you this; the man who climbs into the sheepfold by
some other way, instead of entering by the door, comes to steal and
to plunder: It is the shepherd who tends the sheep that comes in by
the door. At his coming the Keeper of the door throws it open, and
the sheep are attentive to his voice; and so he calls by name the sheep
which belong to him, and leads them out with him. When he has
brought out all the sheep which belong to him, he walks in front of
them, and the sheep follow him, recognizing his voice. If a stranger
comes, they run away from him instead of following him; they cannot recognize the voice of a stranger."

This was a parable which Jesus told to His disciples, but they
did not understand. So Jesus spoke to them again: "Believe me," He
said, "it is I Who am the door of the sheepfold. Those others who
found their way in are all thieves and robbers; to these the sheep paid
no attention. I am the door; a man will find salvation if he makes his
way in through Me; he will come and go at will, and find pasture.
The thief only comes to steal, to slaughter, to destroy; I have come

so that they may have life, and have it more abundantly." These are the words of our dear Lord as Saint John records them. Our Lord said that He was the door of the sheepfold. Now what is this sheepfold of which Christ is the door? It is the heart of the Father. Christ is indeed the precious door that unlocked the loving paternal heart, that adorable heart of God that was locked to all mankind. In the sheepfold all the saints are assembled. The Shepherd is the Eternal Word, the door is Christ's humanity. By the sheep are meant the human souls; yet Angels, too, belong to this fold, and to all rational creatures the Eternal Word has opened the way to that beloved dwelling-place of which He is the Good Shepherd. The Keeper of the Door is the Holy Spirit, for as Saint Ambrose and Saint Jerome tell us, all truth that is received and expressed comes from the Holy Spirit.

We have already mentioned during these days of Pentecost how the Holy Spirit stirs man's heart, how He incites and pursues it relentlessly: Those who inwardly cleave to God understand by experience what is meant by this. How lovingly and tenderly does He unlock the door, which is the Father's heart, and bids them to ceaselessly enter this hidden treasure, the joy and riches of this dwelling-place! It is quite inconceivable and incomprehensible how open, how accessible, how receptive God is, and how He rushes toward us every moment and every hour of the day! Oh, my Beloved, how frequently is this admonition, this loving invitation, this longing ignored; and how needlessly is it rejected. We read in the Book of Esther that King Assuerus invited Queen Vashti to a banquet and bade her to come to him; when the festivities were already in progress, she did not come. He turned her away and rejected her, and banned her forever from his presence; and he chose another, called Esther, in her place. Oh, my Beloved, how many entreaties, how many invitations of the Holy Spirit have we rejected in this way! And all for the sake of created things. God truly desires us while we desire something else.

The Keeper of the Door now calls forth His own sheep, and the Shepherd, too, Who is the Word of the eternal Father, calls them by their name and leads them out. He walks ahead, and they adhere to him. To what place does He lead and call His sheep? To the sheepfold, straight into the heart of the Father, where He has His home, His dwelling, His resting-place. But all who arrive there have to pass through the door, which is Christ in His humanity. His own sheep are those who do not set their heart on anything but God and His voice within them; they seek nothing but His honor and His will, nothing else whatsoever. He walks ahead of them and they follow; they do not follow a stranger from whom they flee and run away. They follow the Shepherd for they know His voice.

Now if Christ Himself tells us that He is the door to the truth, and that those who enter by another way are all thieves and robbers, who then are these thieves? They are those who rely on their own skills and subtle reasoning to enter by that door; who feel no attraction to God, in purity and simplicity of heart; who fail to follow the sweet example of Our Lord Jesus Christ in humble forgetfulness of self, denying themselves in true submission. All these enter the sheepfold by the wrong door.

And who is the thief who steals there? It is a treacherous thorn in human nature, an abominable parasite; it is man's despicable tendency to seize everything, to refer everything to himself, to grasp what he can from God and creatures. Such a man is full of self-will and will do anything to satisfy his own greed. It gives him the illusion that he is all-powerful. He craves pleasure, comforts, thrills, and all manner of experiences; he wishes nothing more than to be grand and glorious and rich. By acquiring power and knowledge, he wants to be somebody, and he never forgets his own importance. That is the thief who sneaks up in his devilish way, depriving God of His honor and man of all truth and perfection. Oh, my Beloved! What a great devastation this thief has produced among mankind, greater than all the thieves who have ever been hanged in the course of time. Take heed, be on your guard, beware!

And who is the robber of whom Christ spoke? It is the unspeakably harmful tendency to pass judgment upon our neighbor. This tendency is deeply rooted in human nature and many people are guilty of it. It is an evil inclination that makes a man willing to always judge others without ever attempting to judge himself. So-and-so, he will say, talks too much; another too little. One man eats too much, another not enough; this one weeps too much, that one ought to weep more. In all circumstances we encounter this destructive judging, and this again gives rise to a deep contempt which shows itself in a person's behavior and speech. Thus one inflicts on one's neighbor the same wound which one bears oneself, by passing the evil judgment on to him. And finally a mortal blow is inflicted on him when all this comes to his hearing.

What do you really know about your neighbor? Do you know what God has willed for him, or to what destiny he has been called? And yet you would like to do his work in your way and dominate him. Do you wish to cast out God's will and improve on it by your own false judgment? Such a murderous action does inconceivable harm among religious persons and they forget that the Lord said: "Judge not that you may not be judged; and what measure you mete, it shall be measured to you again." One should never pass judgment on any action that is not an [external] mortal sin. Should a person, however, be in a position where he is called to pass judgment, then it should be the Holy Spirit Who does it through him: at the right moment, with gentleness and humility, so as not to inflict ten wounds while healing one; not with violence and rashness, but with love and forbearance. If one behaves otherwise, one acts in darkness and not in light.

My Beloved! Know yourselves! Judge yourselves, and realize that all your life you drag around with you a nature full of sin. For this reason you should judge yourself, and allow your neighbor to settle his affairs with God and God with him, if you hope to ever arrive at the sheepfold which is the dwelling-place of all delight. Be sure of one thing: The number of persons above which you have exalted yourself by your judgments and condemnations will be the number of those by whom you shall be brought down.

If a man would only look inward and be himself the robber, what judgment he would then make of himself with a sharp and discerning eye! Soon the robber will discover the thief lurking in the depth, this harmful presumption which has deprived and still is depriving the soul of God, and of His spirit, His grace and that treasure which contains all riches in itself. This thief is now brought to trial before the robber who accuses him of his grave crime; whereupon the robber captures the thief and puts him to death. If only it could happen now, as it often does, that each stabbed the other and both were dead, if the robber and the thief were slain together. What a greatly salutary event that would be! Then all judgments would die and be lost in God, in His will, in His ground, in whichever way He would choose. This would be true and essential peace, if thief and robber both lay dead.

Such a man would be blessed and would enter the sheepfold by the right door. The Doorkeeper would let him enter straight into the abyss of the Father. There he would come and go at will, finding rich pasture everywhere. He would be plunged into the depth of the Godhead in unfathomable bliss, and emerge again into a new humanity which has been divinized by Christ, in deep joy and sweet rejoicing. In him would be realized what Our Lord spoke elsewhere through the Prophet Joel: "I will feed my sheep and I will cause them to lie down." There, activity and rest are all one. "And their pastures shall be in the high mountains of Israel. On the green grass of the Father's pasture I will feed them." This sweet and exalted Shepherd, the eternal Word, shall then walk ahead of His beloved sheep, and they will follow Him, and not a stranger. Hence they will be given in full measure that noble, precious, and delectable food which is nothing else but the sharing of God's blessedness, given to them that they may consume it, savor it, and rejoice in it for all eternity. May God grant that this may be in store for us.

AMEN.

SERMON 29
[FEAST OF THE BLESSED TRINITY II]

Quod scimus loquimur, et quod vidimus testamur
We speak of what we know, and we bear witness to what
we have seen (Jn 3:11)

The second interpretation of the Holy Trinity tells us how
its imageless Image dwells in reality in the inmost ground
of the soul. Here man can find by grace what God possesses by nature, if only he will let himself sink into that
ground, and if he frees himself from all sensual images and
worldly attachments.

Our dear Lord said: "We speak of what we know, and we bear
witness to what we have seen; and our witness you do not receive. If I have spoken of earthly things to you, and you do not believe, how will you believe if I shall speak to you of heavenly things?"
These words are taken from the Gospel of the exalted feast of the
sublime, lofty, and most glorious Trinity. And all the feasts we have
observed throughout the year, whatever they commemorated, have
led up to this one feast and found their consummation in it, just as
the course which creatures run, especially rational creatures, has its
goal and end in the Holy Trinity, for in a sense it is both beginning
and end. When we come to speak of the Most Blessed Trinity, we
are at a loss for words, and yet words must be used to say something
of this sublime and ineffable Trinity. To express it adequately is as
impossible as touching the sky with one's head. For everything we
can say or think can no more approach the reality than the smallest
point of a needle can contain Heaven and earth; indeed, a hundred,
a thousand times, and immeasurably less than that.

It is utterly impossible for our intellect to understand how the lofty, essential Unity can be single in essence and yet threefold in Persons; how the Persons are distinct from each other; how the Father begets the Son; how the Son proceeds from the Father and yet remains within Him (by comprehending Himself the Father utters His Eternal Word); how from this comprehension that proceeds from Him, there streams forth an ineffable love, which is the Holy Spirit; and how these wondrous Processions stream back again in essential unity, in ineffable self-delight and self-enjoyment; how the Son is equal to the Father in power, wisdom, and love; how the Son and the Holy Spirit are also one. And yet there is an inexpressibly vast distinction between the Persons, although they proceed in an ineffable way in unity of nature. On this subject a staggering amount of things could be said, and yet nothing would have been said to convey how the supreme, superabundant Unity unfolds into Trinity.

To experience the working of the Trinity is better than to talk about it. In fact one shies away from a busy scrutiny of this mystery, especially as the words are borrowed from the world as we know it, and also because of the disproportion between the subject and our intelligence to which all this is unutterably high and hidden. For this subject even surpasses the understanding of the Angels. So let us leave the learned discourses to the scholars: They have to engage in them in order to safeguard the Faith. And they have written weighty volumes on the subject. It is for us to believe in simplicity.

Saint Thomas says: "No one should go beyond what those doctors affirmed, who have experienced and pursued these truths at the source, where they have received them from the Holy Spirit." And though there is no subject more joyous and sweet to the taste, there is also nothing more grievous than falling into error concerning it. Therefore stop your disputations on that mystery, and believe it in simplicity, entrusting yourselves wholly to God. Even for the great scholars there is no better way than this, and yet they have never been more subtle in their reasoning than now. You, however, should allow the Holy Trinity to be born in the center of your soul, not by the use of human reason, but in essence and in truth; not in words, but in reality. It is the divine mystery we should seek, and how we are truly its Image; for this divine Image certainly dwells in our souls by nature, actually, truly, and distinctly, though of course not in as lofty a manner as it is in Itself.

Above all, cherish this very sweet Image which dwells in you in such a blessed and unique manner. Nobody can express adequately its nobility, for God is in this Image, indeed He is the Image, in a way which surpasses all our powers of comprehension.

Scholars discuss this Image a great deal, trying to express in various natural ways its nature and essence. They all assert that it belongs to the highest faculties of our soul, which are memory, intellect, and will; that these faculties enable us to receive and enjoy the Blessed Trinity. This is indeed true, but it is the lowest degree of perception, leaving the mystery in the natural order. Saint Thomas says that the perfection of the Image lies in its activity, in the exercise of the faculties; that is, in the active memory, in the active intellect, and in the active will. Further than that Saint Thomas will not go.

Other theologians, however, state—and here we have something of far greater significance—that the Image of the Blessed Trinity rests in the most intimate, hidden, and inmost ground of the soul, where God is present essentially, actively, and substantially. Here God acts and exists and rejoices in Himself, and to separate God from this inmost ground would be as impossible as separating Him from Himself. This is God's eternal decree; He has ordained that He cannot and will not separate Himself. And thus in the depth of this ground the soul possesses everything by grace which God possesses by nature. In the measure in which man surrenders himself and turns to that inmost ground, grace is born in the highest way.

A pagan master, Proclus, has this to say on the subject: "As long as man is occupied with images inferior to himself, and as long as he does not go beyond them, it is unlikely that he will ever reach this depth. It will appear an illusion to really believe that this ground exists within us; we doubt that it can actually exist in us. Therefore," he continues, "if you wish to experience its existence, you must abandon all multiplicity and concentrate your attention on this one thing with the eyes of your intellect; and if you wish to rise higher, you must put aside all rational methods, for reason is now beneath you, and then you may become united with the One." And he calls this state a divine darkness: still, silent, at rest, and above all sense perception.

Beloved, it is a disgraceful thing that a pagan philosopher understood and attained this truth, while we are so far from both. Our Lord expressed the same truth when he said: "The kingdom of God is within us." It is to be found in the inmost depth, beyond the activity of our faculties. And so we read in today's Gospel: "We speak of what we know, and we bear witness to what we have seen; and our witness you do not receive." Indeed, how could a person who lives merely by his senses receive this witness? To those who subscribe to such a way of life, that which is beyond the senses appears as an illusion. As Our Lord says: "As the heavens are exalted above the earth, so are my ways exalted above your ways, and my thoughts above your thoughts." And Our Lord says the same thing today: "If I have spoken to you of earthly things and you believe not, how will you believe if I shall speak to you of heavenly things?" Recently I spoke to you about wounded love, and you said that you could not understand me, and yet we were dealing only with earthly things. How can you then expect to understand things spiritual and divine?

You are concerned with so many external affairs, always busy with one thing or another; this is not the witness of which Our Lord said: "We bear witness to what we have seen." This witness is to be found in your inmost ground, beyond sensual images; within this ground the Heavenly Father begat His only-begotten Son, swifter a million times than the twinkling of an eye. And this happens in the swiftness of eternity that is forever new, in the inexplicable splendor of His own Being. Whoever wishes to experience this must turn inward, far beyond his exterior and interior faculties, beyond all that the imagination has ever acquired from outside, so that he may sink and melt into that ground. Then the power of the Father will come and call the soul into Himself through His only-begotten Son, and as the Son is born of the Father and returns into Him, so man is born of the Father in the Son, and flows back into the Father through the Son, becoming one with Him. Thus Our Lord says: "You will call me Father and will not cease to walk after me. This day have I begotten you, through and in my Son." And now the Holy Spirit pours Himself out in inexpressible and overflowing love and joy, flooding and saturating the ground of the soul with His wondrous gifts.

Two of these may be called active gifts, namely, piety and knowledge. They make man kind and gentle. And the gift of knowledge allows him to discern what way is best for him. But the corresponding virtues must have preceded these gifts, for the gifts now bestowed lead man into a state beyond the exercise of virtues.

Next come the passive gifts, and they go hand in hand: fortitude and counsel. The third gift, fear, faces inward, for it protects and strengthens what the Holy Spirit has worked. Finally come the two highest gifts, understanding, and the wisdom that is a taste of God.

Beloved, the devil lays snares for such people, they are tempted by those demons who are the craftiest and most subtle. Therefore such men are in great need of the gift of discerning knowledge. To remain in that state of interior union for just one second is worth more than all exterior works and rules; and it is in the depth of this ground that we should pray for our friends, living or dead. That would be far more efficacious than reciting a hundred thousand Psalters.

This, then, is the true witness: "The Holy Spirit, testifying to our spirit that we are the children of God." And thus we receive this testimony in our hearts, as it says in today's Gospel. In Heaven, that means in the heaven within our soul, there are three who bear witness: the Father, the Word, and the Spirit. They are your witnesses who give the true testimony that you are a child of God. They illuminate the depth of your ground, and thus your own ground becomes your witness. And this witness also testifies against you and against all the disorders within you; and this testimony enlightens your reason, whether you like it or not, and reveals your whole life to you, if you will only listen. Listen carefully to this testimony and live accordingly if you wish to be saved at the Day of Judgment. If you reject it by your words and deeds and by your whole life, the same witness will condemn you at the last day and that will be your fault and not God's. Beloved, always listen to this witness within, and you will never regret it.

You have sailed down the Rhine in order to take up a life of poverty. But if you fail to reach this ground within you, no amount of traveling will get you there. Do not waste your energy! Shed all outward attachments, turn inward, and seek the deepest ground of your soul; exterior precepts and techniques will be of no avail. In the lives of the Fathers we read of a good husband who fled into the forest to avoid these obstacles; he had as many as two thousand brethren under his care, all seeking this same interior ground. And his wife had a community of many under her care. This ground, however, is a single, hidden solitude, utterly sublime, a darkness forever accessible to your free will. No path of the senses will ever lead you there. And then you will say: "I love spiritual people and would like nothing better than helping those who have felt God's touch and have received interior illumination." Whoever draws such people away from the higher graces, enforcing exterior practices upon them, prepares a terrible judgment for himself. Trying to force such souls into pious exercises puts more obstacles in their way than did the pagans and the Jews. And so I warn you, who are so ready to judge with cutting remarks and disdainful gestures, to be indeed careful in dealing with such spiritual people.

And now, if you wish to contemplate the Holy Trinity within you, keep these three points in mind. First, keep God alone before your eyes, His honor, and not your own. Secondly, in all your works and exterior activities keep a close watch over yourself; be constantly mindful of your utter nothingness, and observe carefully what occupies you most. Thirdly, ignore what goes on around you: If it is not your business, do not pay attention to it; it will take care of itself. If things are good, let them be so; if they seem bad, do not criticize and ask questions. Turn into the depth of your ground and remain there, so that you may hear the voice of the Father Who calls you. He calls you to Himself and endows you with such riches that, if it were necessary, you could answer all the questions of the entire clergy in the Church; of such clarity and brilliance are the gifts God bestows upon His lovers.

And should you forget everything that has been said here, keep in mind these two little points: First, be truly humble, throughout your whole being, not only in mind and in outward conduct; think lowly of yourself, and see yourself honestly for what you are. And secondly, let the love you bear God be a true one; not just what is usually understood by the term, which refers only to emotions, but a love that embraces God most ardently. Such love is a far cry from what is usually meant by religious feeling, which is situated in the senses. What I mean here transcends all sensible experience; it is a gazing upon God with one's entire spirit, a being drawn by love, just as a runner is drawn, or an archer, who has a single goal before his eyes.

May the Blessed Trinity grant us to arrive at this inmost ground where its true image dwells.

AMEN.

SERMON 33

[FEAST OF CORPUS CHRISTI IV]

Caro mea vere est cibus et sanguis meus vere est potus
My flesh is truly food, and My blood is truly drink
(Jn 6:55)

The fourth interpretation of the Blessed Sacrament treats
of two kinds of obstacles, one habitual, the other occasional. Both hinder man's spiritual progress, so that he cannot receive the benefits of the Lord's Supper. Those sins
which appear repeatedly, some graver than others, are
given individual attention.

"My flesh is truly food, and My blood is truly drink." Yesterday I said I wanted to speak about the glory of the Blessed
Sacrament—though no one can adequately do so—about its benefits
and how we should prepare for its reception; but I did not manage
to speak about preparation. Although all this far exceeds our human
faculties, we can still conclude a little from what Saint Thomas tells
us. He says that all the glory and grace and blessedness which Our
Lord brought to the world through His humanity, His life and death
and Passion, His Resurrection and Ascension, all these He brings to
every man in the Blessed Sacrament. There is no imaginable gift any
man can desire which is not contained and included in it.

You may ponder this as profoundly, as loftily, and as devoutly
as you will: All the exercises of piety which man can perform by his
own powers are as nothing compared with it; godly they may be,
but this sacrament is God Himself; in it man is transformed in God
by grace, as Saint Augustine was told by Our Lord. "You shall not
change me into yourself, but into Me you shall be changed." What-

ever it is that you could ever want or desire, to conquer your failings, obtain graces or virtues, consolation or love, you will find it all here, if only you seek it in the right way. Even if a man had lived a hundred years and had committed a hundred or a thousand mortal sins. Every day—if God granted him a true conversion from his sins, so that he would go to the Lord's table with this disposition, then it would be easy for Our Lord to forgive him all his sins in an instant with this high and noble gift of Himself; as easy as it would be for you to blow a fleck of dust off your hand; and this conversion could be so powerful that all pain and penance would be at once wiped away, and this man could become a great saint.

Here in Cologne people are in the habit of receiving the Body of Our Lord frequently, and this is a good thing; but they do not all receive it in the same way. Some do indeed receive the Host, but not spiritually with their whole soul, and they do so in a state of mortal sin, as Judas did. Others again receive it sacramentally as well as spiritually, but they gain little grace, benefit, or consolation; they are the ones who receive it with many venial sins on their conscience, and they lack preparation and devoutness. Others receive it with immense spiritual benefit and infinite profit; and there are those who receive it spiritually, without actual sacramental communion, good people, pure in heart, who long for the Blessed Sacrament, but to whom it cannot be given at the time. These latter perhaps receive the grace of the sacrament in a higher degree, in proportion to their desire and disposition, than those who receive it sacramentally.

A good man may do this a hundred times a day, wherever he may be, in sickness or in health. Although one cannot receive the Body of Our Lord sacramentally more than once a day, one can receive it spiritually, through holy desire and in a devout spirit with immeasurable grace and profit. If one receives the Blessed Sacrament always with the right disposition, the soul will derive great benefit in eternal life, supposing God grants one to be free of sin at the hour of death. Yet such people never know the sweet outpouring of love and the innumerable graces which flow from it, because they come to a standstill at outward observances and pass through life superficially, without being able to rid themselves of their daily sins. They approach the Lord's Table in a lukewarm manner, and they leave it graceless, empty, dull, and cold, and because of these great obstacles they make no progress.

What, then, are the obstacles which cause such incomparable harm, depriving people of the precious bounty which fills heaven and earth with its riches while they themselves remain empty and unfulfilled? It is a state we can observe all around us. You must understand that these venial sins let works of love grow cold, dissipate the affections, drive out and hinder devotion, take away spiritual consolation, and destroy the intimacy between God and man by bringing about an alienation. Even if such sins do not essentially destroy grace, they nevertheless do great damage by creating situations in which one is apt to lose it by falling into grave sin. Such is the harm that merely venial sins can cause.

Such daily venial sins are of two kinds: Some are habitual, others occasional. Of whichever kind they are, they hinder the sweet graces of the Blessed Sacrament from flowing into the soul. Yet we must draw a distinction: The habitual sins, which present a great stumbling-block to many of us, consist in our yielding willfully and knowingly to created things—whatever their nature, animate or inanimate—and placing our love and satisfaction in them for their own sake, without reference to God.

Beloved, to crave and find satisfaction in the senses belongs to venial sin, and frequently it is so great that one condemns oneself to long years in purgatory in order to atone for it. Such sins are so deeply rooted that man is unwilling to give up creatures and the satisfactions derived from them for the love of God; the result is that created things occupy the place of God in man, so that God can neither dwell nor do His work there.

For this reason everyone should take a close look at himself and see whether there is any disordered self-love or perhaps any inordinate love, be it of one's family or one's wife. Alas, my Beloved, such sin is very common nowadays. Everybody seeks to amass possessions, and hoard them, becoming more and more greedy in the process. We can observe this attitude among the clergy as well as in the world; nobody is satisfied with what he has, everybody thinks he must acquire more, and so people build themselves huge edifices and decorate them in foolish ways; they crowd them with all kinds of curiosities to distract their senses, silver goblets and services and rich ornaments, all sorts of luxurious fashions. And all this display exists for pleasure and ostentation only.

In that way they strengthen their habitual daily sins, encouraging the greed that exists in them. Sometimes they suffer from boredom, and then they crave society to distract and amuse them. But in all this they do not seek God, they are not mindful of Him, and they do not find Him. Alas, my Beloved, how closely related are such things to the deadly damage of mortal sin, inwardly and outwardly! Before one knows it, one has fallen into it.

My Beloved: These are the habitual obstacles with which many of us approach the Lord's Supper. And everyone wants to cling to his ways, refusing to give up any of his attachments. As a result such people feel neither God's presence nor their own enjoyment; but they give no thought to this and turn their attention again to their beloved possessions. And yet many of them have been wearing a religious habit for forty or fifty years. It is questionable indeed whether they will be saved at the Day of Judgment, for their spirit is habitually chained to created things and willfully entangled in them. You may be sure that such people are not aware of their state. Of course they find numerous excuses: "I must have such and such a thing," they will say. "Surely, it will do me no harm." And thus they offer these obstacles a seat within themselves, and there they unite with their natural inclinations to such a degree that they can no longer feel any compunction and so they ignore them. These are strong and powerful obstacles, veritable fortresses erected against God's work, and yet such people are not even aware of them. For in the measure in which man is possessed by created things, God and His graces must turn away.

Then there are the occasional sins. Who falls into them? People who are not necessarily obsessed or enslaved by created things, animate or inanimate; indeed they are always ready to give up what is displeasing to God, people or friendships or possessions, as long as they are convinced that this is what God asks them to do. And yet they are not as much on their guard as they ought to be, for they are inclined by nature to be overcome by their weaknesses. These may be of any sort: anger, pride, inertia, frivolous talk. If the occasion arises, they yield to these inclinations, and thus they talk or drink or eat too much, or fall into excess in their amusements and other activities. These sins are of the graver sort, but if they are committed from human weakness and thoughtlessness, they present less serious encumbrances to grace because the heart remains pure, although the lack of prudence is deplorable.

However, if a man intends to approach the Lord's Table today or tomorrow and does not guard against these things, such neglect will surely hinder that loving meeting and union with God; it will diminish trust, disperse and distract the mind, and render him unreceptive to the glorious light which should transfigure and flood his soul.

If these sins had been committed yesterday, without design, and one is bitterly sorry for them today, then they are not as great a hindrance as if they had happened today; for the bitterness of sorrow cleanses away much of the rust left by sin.

Still, if such a person is as careless today as he was yesterday, and if he allows himself to be distracted by idle talk and wastes his time by all kinds of disordered activities, that would be more serious and lead to an accumulation of sin. Nevertheless, we must not abstain from receiving the Blessed Sacrament because of it; we do not sin by receiving it, if only we are sorry for our sins and resolve to do better tomorrow.

Nature, too, may lead to improper attitudes by such things as excessive sleep or food. We should sometimes try to get by with only a mouthful, and see whether our nature can endure it. Beloved, if God should pour forth His infinite holiness into us, we must be utterly pure, or the secret treasury of the divine goodness cannot flow into us unimpeded.

Sometimes good, pure-hearted people may be sluggish and apathetic without wanting to be. Their nature demands more sleep than they like to admit, but this is no reason for abstaining from Holy Communion. It is different with those who seek nothing but their own gratification: If they do not experience emotional comfort, a sense of security, and a warm glow, they stay away from the sacrament entirely. Instead of seeking God, they seek only themselves. Such people God often leaves to their own devices, allowing heavy blows to fall upon them, and they will be afflicted by great anguish, so that it will seem to them that they are suffering the pain of hell. And if no such trials should come upon them, then you may be sure that their punishment in purgatory will be great indeed. People like this make no progress; they remain the same to the end of their days. Nothing is to be expected from them.

Others again are good men, but so gripped by fear that they dare not approach the Table of Our Lord unless they actually can feel the fire of love or experience the divine action with their senses. Although they are not aware of any obstacle, they, too, make no progress.

Those, however, who find the depth of their soul and their intentions pure and whose aspirations are directed wholly toward God will receive the greatest fruits from the Blessed Sacrament; nothing will put them off, nothing will shatter their trust in God, no matter what He sends them or takes away from them. They are born in Him and He in them; if they encounter an obstacle arising from their own nature or from circumstances, they quickly overcome it without wasting time in scruples. It is God they love, and it is Him they have in mind. They sink into Him, seeking not His gifts but Him only; they accept all things from Him and refer them back to Him again. In such men the Blessed Sacrament effects a noble and glorious transformation, and for them it is the shortest and quickest way.

A person like this could receive the Blessed Sacrament with such great devotion that, if he were about to join the lowest choir of Angels, he would by this one communion be granted to be taken up into the second, third, or fourth. If he would take the Lord's Supper frequently, he could rise to the highest choir, beyond cherubim and seraphim, surpassing even the nature of Angels. This, however, man should not seek, but only desire the blessed will of God and his honor. The wonders which are effected by this sacrament in the depth of a truly purified soul are far beyond the comprehension of Angels and men, for the soul is now lifted above itself and all human ways, drawn into God and united to Him.

If it happens that such a person is unable to partake of this gift sacramentally, he should resign himself to partake of it spiritually. He should do this at least once a day, whether he can hear Mass or not.

My Beloved! What wonders we could work with God's help if we would turn into our depths and remain there and avail ourselves of the grace that is in us! We would find true freedom and the Kingdom of God within. But that is exactly what we fail to do; we look for all things outside ourselves, pursuing this and that, and in this process we finally lose ourselves. It is not different with you! You very diligently have come to listen to my sermon, you have heard the Word of God, and before you know it, you have forgotten it. Now you will be off to listen to another preacher, and soon you will not know what either of them has said. You turn to exterior things again, and there is no end of trouble. We are unstable people, you and I, unsteady and inconstant.

I have visited countries where people act in a strong manner, persevering in their conversion with steadfastness. There the Word of God produces more fruit in a single year than it does here in ten. Marvels of divine grace can be observed among these splendid people. In other countries again we find people with a weak disposition. Whatever their opportunities, nothing comes of them. You do not like to hear this said about you, but we must all act in a vigorous manner, turning our direction away from creatures and toward God, or nothing will come of us. What a miserable thing it is to see God's infinite grace squandered so carelessly! It is enough to break one's heart.

Unfortunately there are some religious communities where there is altogether too much talk going on; what this or that one has said or done, or what the latest news is. Such nonsense can hinder the soul's union with God. Those, however, who really want to hear and speak of God cannot get a good reception there. I beg you to keep away from such places and such conversations; retire to your room, open your heart to God and His will, and then follow it! And if God's will is hidden from you, take this advice from me: If you have to choose between two courses of action, what to accept and what to renounce, and you are not sure which one is the more pleasing to God, look into your own heart, and then do what is less pleasing to your nature. If you choose what appeals to your natural inclinations, you will be less safe. The more you live for natural satisfactions, the less you live for God and His will; the more you want to live in the spirit, the more you must learn to die to self.

This is what I wished to tell you about the glory of this incomparable sacrament. It falls far short of what one would like to say. One would like to speak of its benefit and of its efficacy, of the glory it gives to God, the joy it presents to the saints, and all it contributes to the betterment of mankind, to the conversion of mortal sinners, and the release of souls from purgatory.

We read that a friend of God once had a vision of a soul wrapped in flames, like a burning torch; the soul in torment said that the insufferable agonies were due to his negligence in receiving the Body of Our Lord. "But," he added, "if you will only receive Our Lord's Body and Blood with devotion once for me, that will bring me help." This the friend of God did; and the next day the soul appeared to Him again, more resplendent and glorious than the sun. Because of this one Holy Communion it had been freed from its unbearable pains, and taken up at once into eternal life.

May God give us all the grace to live a good life! May the Father, the Son, and the Holy Spirit grant us this gift.

AMEN.

SERMON 35

[THIRD SUNDAY AFTER TRINITY I]

Carissimi, humilamini sub potenti manu Dei
Beloved, humble yourselves under the mighty hand of
God (1 Pt 5:6)

This Sermon takes its text from Saint Peter's Epistle for the
Third Sunday after Trinity. It teaches the three virtues of
humility, love of God, and prudence and how to be on
guard against the roaring lion, the devil.

"Beloved, humble yourselves, therefore, under the mighty hand of God, that He may exalt you in the time of visitation; cast all your anxiety upon Him, because He cares for you. Be sober, be watchful! For your adversary, the devil, as a roaring, growling lion, goes about seeking someone to devour. Resist him, steadfast in the Faith, knowing that the same suffering befalls your brothers all over the world. But the God of all grace, who has called us to His eternal glory, will see you through and make you strong and firm in Jesus Christ, to Whose honor you now endure these little pains. To Him be honor forever."

This is the letter which our dear prince of the Apostles, Saint Peter, puts before us. It contains an entire doctrine which enables us to carry out and perfect what Holy Church has shown us throughout the year in all her feasts. Everything is summed up and brought to conclusion in this letter, if we give Saint Peter's teaching serious thought.

He said: "Dear brothers, beloved, humble yourselves under the mighty hand of God." You must observe here three virtues which everyone must possess and toward which our religious practices, our conduct, our entire life must be directed. If any of these is missing,

117

then our conduct, our life, and all our practices will be of no value whatsoever. The first thing Saint Peter wants us to do is to humble ourselves beneath God. That is the foundation on which rests the whole edifice of our lives and our actions; without it, everything is bound to collapse.

The second virtue is true love of God, the third is prudence. With the aid of these three, man is able to attain every other perfection.

Now God, who is all-loving and merciful, has implanted these virtues in the very depths of our nature, knowing how greatly we are in need of them. He placed them in our innermost core, thereby making us His close kin. I am speaking of the noble spark of the soul, divinely hued, more intimate and closer to us than we are to ourselves. And yet, for all that, it is strange and unknown to us. This is due to our pride. If our nature were harmoniously ordered, we should constantly be able to activate these virtues; with their aid we could free ourselves from self-love if we were only willing and refused to be distracted.

In regard to humility, we find both cause and reason for it in two conditions which affect our spiritual and outward life alike: our natural frailty and our inclination to sin. In order to realize this, we need only observe how inadequate our nature is, always craving things, always consuming them, and all ending in nothing. We are only too familiar with this aspect of our human nature. We come from nothing, and to nothing we shall return. The second reason for humility lies in our tendency to sin. If only we could remain within ourselves and look deeply into our nature, we would realize this abysmal tendency to sin and the enormous extent of our exposure to it. We should understand how feeble and flawed we are, how bent on evil without end, in quite an incomprehensible way. This tendency is bound to lead to eternal damnation among the evil spirits. Is this not reason enough to be humble? After some introspection we are bound to observe that our nature points toward humility, considering how great our deficiencies are.

The second virtue is true love of God, which is deeply implanted and embedded in human nature. Man's love arises from his nature. It is not so with humility, which has to come to us from outside. Love, however, is firmly rooted. Bede says that it would be as impossible for man to live without love as to live without a soul. If man's nature were harmoniously ordered, he would have to love God more than he loves himself. What a sad pity it is to so pervert our nobility that our love is turned to creatures and not to Him Who created them.

The third virtue is prudence, which arises from reason, because man is a rational creature. Be assured that anything you do which is not governed by prudence will not be good, because it is not pleasing to God. This is why Saint Peter tells us in his Epistle to be sober and watchful. It means that prudence should soberly guide and govern every man's words and actions and his whole life: in all places and in all his relations, always and in every way, inwardly and outwardly.

Now let us return again to the first virtue: "Humble yourselves under the mighty hand of God, that He may exalt you in the time of visitation." If God, in the time of visitation, finds our soul devoid of humility, we shall be in a bad way. For we read in Scripture that God hates the proud, but gives His grace to the humble. The greater the humility of man, the greater the grace of God; the less the humility, the less the grace. And if He finds us proud, you may be sure that He will bring us low; if He finds us lowly, He will raise us up, for lowliness creates exaltation. It is for this reason that we should be humbled and abased. God's hand is so mighty, so wise and good and loving; we, however, are weak and blind and inclined to evil. Without Him we can do nothing.

Therefore Saint Peter said: "Cast all your anxiety upon Him, because He cares for you." Even if we received from God no other benefits, no other help than His daily care, which shields us from so many spiritual and temporal sorrows, preserving us from afflictions of heart and body, forever comforting and liberating: If only we remained within ourselves, we would soon become aware of God, and this ought to be enough to draw and attract us to Him. And although all things exist in Him in [undifferentiated] Unity, this need not cause us fear: Whatever happens to us individually is ordained and foreseen by Him in exactly that way and no other.

Saint Peter continues: "Be sober and watchful!" When the adversary, the lion, roars with his dreadful voice, the other beasts fall down in fright; then the lion seizes and devours them. In the same manner the adversary falls upon us small, frail creatures, and if we are not sufficiently rooted, we fall down at once and let him devour us. Now Saint Peter tells us to be watchful and resist the devil's onslaught bravely with our Faith.

JOHANNES TAULER

We must behave as people do in a besieged city: they watch where the attackers are strongest and the defenses weakest. If they fail to do this, the city is lost. In the same manner we should keep our eyes carefully on the point where the devil most often attacks us, where human nature is weakest, where our frailties lie, and here we should keep guard most vigilantly.

Now the devil is apt to cause confusion and despondency. When we consider our natural weakness and our tendency to sin, it fills us with depression and anxiety. Then along comes the lion, the devil, and whispers: "Are you going to spend your life in grief and sorrow? What folly! Enjoy yourself as others do, and get some pleasure out of life. God will give you plenty of time to repent at the end. Do what pleases you, and enjoy the world while you can. Time enough to become a saint when you are old."—Oh, my Beloved! Take good care while the day lasts, so that the darkness may not catch you unawares; be sober and watchful and remember that you pass through this life only once. Be on your guard that those plants of which Our Lord spoke will not be found in you: "The plants which my Father in Heaven has not planted must be torn out by the roots." Beloved, consider all this wisely.

The devil's insinuations can take so many forms: "Oh," people will say to themselves, "if only I had a spiritual director. The thoughts that come to my mind! What a mess I am." Well, I know a lot about these thoughts, and my advice to you is this: What the devil has put in your mind, you can put out again. Be at peace, turn your heart to God, pay no attention to such disturbing thoughts, do not dwell on them and let them pass out of your mind. You will often experience perplexity of this kind, which is all the doing of the devil and comes from this excessive despondency. In the end he will drive you to despair, so that you may exclaim: "It is all hopeless anyway!" How should you act then? Cast all your anxiety on God! Be solidly anchored in Him. When sailors are in danger of running aground and all seems to be lost, they throw their anchor overboard and it sinks to the bottom of the Rhine; that is the way they defend themselves against danger. And it is the way we, too, should act: When we are assailed by grave temptations of mind and body, we should abandon all else and let the anchor sink deep into the ground, which means perfect trust in God's fidelity. In similar situations, the sailors let oars and rudder go and firmly seize the anchor. That is what is required if you find yourself in distress of body or soul of any kind.

If only we could seize the anchor at the time of our death and so die in perfect hope and trust, what a blessed death it would be! We ought to cultivate trust in God the way we cultivate the other virtues, to aid us at the moment of death. I am not talking about a false trust. For a person to live an evil life and then to trust in God is a sin against the Holy Spirit, because evil done with full knowledge and consent presumes upon God's mercy in the future.

No, the trust I am speaking of springs from the depth of true humility and love. It is based on the awareness that we can do nothing by ourselves, and with right judgment we entrust ourselves to God. Do this joyfully, in total self-surrender, for God loves a joyful giver. Should you not put your trust in Him who has done you such infinite and great good? Even before you were conceived, He knew of your weakness; He knew that you would fall into sin, and He foresaw the manner in which your sins should be wiped away, by His noble death. And this inestimable good He confers upon you day by day, every hour, unceasingly. Turn away from all else and turn wholly to Him. Know that, whatever temptations you may encounter, as long as you waver, standing there undecided, the devil will never let go of you, and you might easily be defeated.

Are you intent upon overcoming evil? Then turn your back steadfastly on everything that is not God, telling Him with all your heart that you will not sin again. The victory will be yours, and the devil will be put shamefully to flight. For a man to give in to the devil can be compared to a well-armed soldier running away from a fly. We possess much stronger weapons than he: our holy Faith, the Blessed Sacrament, the Word of God, the examples of the saints, the prayers of Holy Church, and much besides. Compared to all this, the devil is weaker than a fly. What we must do is resist him bravely and sink our anchor firmly into God, Who has conferred such great good on us.

Be on your guard: When the time comes to enter the next world, you must have withstood the devil, or you will fall into his hands. He will give you little recompense for having followed him; and then there will be no turning back. Furthermore, we should give constant attention to that ground in our souls, with all the diligence we can bring to bear. How easy it is to slip into a life of perverted values and self-deception. We believe that God can be deceived as we deceive others, and so we waste our precious time and the grace of God. If we do this, God permits the devil to prevent our doing any good.

Take heed while the day lasts and you have light to see by; walk in the light and take care that the darkness does not overtake you; look into your soul in a steadfast and spiritual way.

But there are many who fail in this because all their actions are externalized. If the depths of their souls are touched, they immediately take off and flee to another town or country. By always attempting something new, nothing is ever accomplished and they often run into destruction. They will want to live a life of poverty, withdraw into a hermitage, enter a monastery. It is a good thing for people to enter monastic life, provided they join an approved order and live under the protection of its Rule. They certainly have chosen the safest path, far safer than following their own rules. Even though not all those who enter religion do so from a genuine religious motive, but once they find themselves there they say: "Lord, I give you thanks for having brought me here; I will always serve you, thank and praise you, whatever my reasons for having come here may have been." You may be sure that the most trivial, insignificant work performed in such a spirit of true obedience is better, more praiseworthy and profitable than all the great works a man can perform when he follows his own will.

When a person wishes to take up a new task or a new way of life, let him submit it all to the loving will of God, seeking nothing but God's greater glory in it. Let him examine carefully the measure of God's grace, the purity of his intention, the perfection of his obedience and, finally, whether he is able to carry out the burden the task will demand of him. Let him acknowledge his own insufficiency and look into the depth of his soul, waiting patiently and without distraction to see if he can truly discover in himself a living humility, love, and prudence. If he possesses these three virtues, God may work great and exalted things in him.

Saint Peter teaches that we suffer the same as do our brothers in the world. Beloved, no one can escape suffering. Wherever a person may be, he must suffer. Even those who serve the devil in the world do not escape it. Many a fine fellow, proud and strong, has risked his life in the service of the world and has lost it. What was his reward? His body went to the worms and his soul to the devil. That is what he had to show for it. So be glad to suffer for the sake of God, Who will give you Himself, His kingdom, and eternal life and Who has known suffering Himself. And since the Head knew suffering, it would indeed be shameful for the members to have avoided it altogether.

Is there anyone, anyone, who suffers as much as our dear Lord, Who endures shame and blasphemy every day? If it were possible for Him to suffer as He once did, He would suffer more today than He did when He was crucified. How many times is He crucified again by the terrible oaths sworn upon His death and His wounds? His Passion is daily renewed by the mortal sins that are committed; His wounds are reopened and make his Precious Blood flow again. Think of the shame inflicted upon Him every day when His pure, blessed, divine Body is received into so many foul, stinking, devilish vessels. We are the vessels, and we fill them wittingly with worldly and created things. And if He could still feel the torment He felt on earth, it would hurt Him more to be received by such people than it once hurt to be received by Judas. For they know that He is their God and Creator, which Judas did not. If those who love God could experience physically the pain they feel in their loving hearts for Him, their hearts would be wounded and their souls pierced to the very marrow. They would gladly prefer death to seeing their beloved Lord and God receiving such insult and dishonor.

This, my Beloved, is, in a concentrated form, the true and safe path taught to us by Saint Peter. He told us to humble ourselves. This humility is the foundation on which we are to erect the edifice of love, reason, and prudence. Then God will exalt us in the time of visitation.

There are many who have raised themselves up, using their reason in a worldly way, glorying in the gifts of their superior minds; they have not traveled along this path. They will tumble down and crash into the abyss. The higher the mountain, the deeper the valley.

May God grant us that we shall be found in the true ground, so that He may exalt us and say: "Friend, come up higher."

AMEN.

SERMON 37

[THIRD SUNDAY AFTER TRINITY III]

Quae mulier habens dragmas decem . . .
Or what woman having ten drachmas . . .(Lk 15,8)

This Sermon, based on a text from Saint Luke, deals with the lost coin. It mentions the various manners of burning love, the two different ways in which we should seek God, and how God seeks us by withdrawing all sensible pleasures.

Today I have preached to you on the Gospel passage which relates how the sinners drew near to Our Lord, and how the sheep was lost and sought and found again.

Beloved, look at it any way you want, you must become alike to the sheep in true humility and silence; you must resemble them in noble resignation and in willingness to accept affliction, so that you may be submissive to God and through Him suffer all creatures with a patient spirit. God may wish to seek you in one way or another, through Himself or through men, through the Evil One or through all creatures in Heaven and on earth: Do not justify yourself by harsh words and aggressive actions, no matter how rashly you may be attacked. In this you should follow the very sweet example of Our Lord Jesus Christ Who was the meekest of lambs and did not open His mouth when He was led to the shearer.

Remember that you will be shorn by hard words and many trials by which the Lord wishes to seek you. You will then become alike to Him, a sweet lamb which He will lay on His shoulders and lead it on high, from His sacred humanity, in which you followed Him faithfully, to the divine Being itself, where there is abiding pasture. This is the one thing necessary. Beloved, today's Gospel tells of a woman who has lost a coin, and lit a lantern and searched for it.

This woman signifies God's divinity; the lantern, the humanity of Our Lord divinized; and the coin the soul of man.

A coin must have three characteristics in order to be a proper coin: It must be of the right weight, it must be struck of the right metal, and finally it must bear the proper seal and image. These three conditions must be fulfilled. Also, it must be made of gold or silver, for this is the proper metal for a coin.

My Beloved, what a marvelous thing such a coin is! It is indeed a golden coin and it is unfathomable and incomprehensible in its splendor. It must be of the right weight: but how can one weigh what is immeasurable? It weighs more than heaven and earth and everything contained in it. For God dwells in this coin and hence it weighs as much as God Himself.

Then there is the imprint of the coin, God's divinity printed into it, so deeply that its inexpressible love overflows into man's spirit, sinking into it, and at the same time utterly absorbing and engulfing it. If this is to happen to you, then you must choose a closer and more direct path, one that goes far beyond any exterior exercises of the outer man, be they passive or active, a path transcending all rational analysis. How can this be? Observe what the woman did: She lit a lantern and turned the house upside down.

It was Eternal Wisdom which lit the lantern, and it was lit by God's true love; for a lantern should be ignited and aflamed. Beloved! You do not know what love is. You believe you have found it, because you experience powerful emotions, and feel joy and delight; but this is not love at all. This is not how love behaves. When we love we are aflame, desiring God, lacking God, feeling forsaken by God, in constant torment, yet content to be tormented; consumed by the fire of our thirst for God, and yet, through it all, content. This is love, quite different from what you imagined it to be; it is the lantern ignited.

The woman then turns her house upside down, searching for the coin. How does this search happen within us? One way is active, in which we are seeking; the other passive, in which we are sought. This searching in which we ourselves are involved happens in two different ways. One is exterior, the other interior, and the interior way is as far above the other as Heaven is above earth. We seek God exteriorly when we perform pious practices and good works of various kinds as we are admonished or urged by God, and advised by His friends, mostly by exercising virtues such as humility, gentleness, silence, detachment, and all the other virtues which we practice or can practice.

The other way, however, is far more sublime. We must allow ourselves to sink into our ground, into the innermost depth, and seek the Lord there, as He instructed us when He said: "The Kingdom of God is within you!" Whoever wishes to discover this Kingdom—where God reigns with all His riches in His very essence and nature—he must look for it where it is: in the very depth of the soul, where God is infinitely closer to the soul, more inherent, as the soul is to itself.

This ground, however, must be sought, and it must be found. When we enter this house, everything that pertains to our sense perceptions must be left outside: all images and forms, everything which our imagination has ever acquired from the outside, all fantasms and rational distinctions, even discursive reason itself must be renounced. As soon as we enter our house to search for God there, God in His turn searches for us, and the house is turned upside down. He acts just the way we do when we search for something: throwing aside one thing after another, until we find what we are looking for.

This is precisely what happens in our case: When we have entered our house, and when we have searched for God in the innermost ground, God comes and searches for us and turns our house completely upside down.

Now I would like to express an idea not everyone will understand, though I always speak plain German. Those who have caught a glimpse of what I am speaking about and have been enlightened, those alone will comprehend what I am about to say.

When I speak of entering this house, I do not mean entering it occasionally, only to leave it again and to busy oneself with created things.

If God seeks us and turns this house upside down, all the modes and manners which have enabled us in the past to form a rational concept of Him must be abandoned, if He is going to take possession of this innermost ground. Everything must be reversed so radically as if we had never had any concept of God at all. And as He seeks us, this entire process has to be repeated again and again. All the concepts we have ever formed of Him, all manifestations and revelations, will be turned upside down while He searches for us. And if our nature could endure this reversal, day and night, a thousand times over, and if we could suffer it and surrender to it, then this would be more salutary than all the understanding and all the spiritual sweetness we have tasted up to this moment. Such a reversal, if we submit to it utterly, will lead a man infinitely higher than all the good works and spiritual exercises and endeavors he had devised for himself.

Those who truly achieve this become the most blessed of men, and they can now turn inward at will, in a lightning flash, soaring above their natural state. However, most people are likely to persevere in their earthbound state, clinging to it tightly. And others are so stubbornly attached to their worldly ways that they can be compared to a barn floor which has to be prepared for the threshing: It is so rough and uneven that it needs scrubbing with a strong, stiff broom to even it out. If a threshing floor is already smooth, then it only takes a feather duster to make it shiny. It is the same with people who are crude and uneven and unregenerate; they are in need of God's strong and stiff broom, trials and temptations of all kinds, to teach them how to surrender to Him. Those blessed men, however, who are pure of heart and utterly detached, they have no need of this. They are born anew, for created things have no claim on them, and they sink ever deeper into the divine ground, stripped of creatureliness, truly detached and forgetful of self.

If your spirit were naked and blind and freed of the finite, as the Lord would have it, and if this reversal we have spoken of had been truly effected, then the coin would have been found; and this discovery would exceed all our powers of comprehension.

Ah, my Beloved! Whoever would abandon himself to this process would far transcend all the mighty works and achievements which the whole world could devise. Our Lord assured us of this when He said: "If anyone wishes to follow Me, let him deny himself and come to Me." We must deny ourselves and never come to a standstill at anything which would impede our progress to God.

Now when people who have never learned this self-denial find themselves face-to-face with afflictions, and feel the strokes of God's hand, their tribulations become worse than before, and they fall into grave doubt and dismal despair. And then they say: "No, Lord, it is all useless; I have become deprived of all grace and light." If only your spirit were simple and resigned, you would never be more joyous than now that the Lord is searching for you. You would be rich enough and in possession of an abiding peace. If it were God's wish to find you in blindness or darkness, in the heat of fervor or in coldness and despondency, in poverty or whatever He deigned to decree: Whichever way He searched for you, you would allow Him to find you there.

If man would only adhere to this way and let himself fall into God's arms, how, do you think, God would deal with him then? Ah, He would lovingly lead him beyond all created things.

My dear good people, do not be afraid. There is many a man who lives on water and on good coarse bread; he will arrive where he wants to go. Unless you wish to travel a higher road, you need not concern yourselves with what I am saying.

We have mentioned before that this coin must be of the right weight and bear the proper imprint. The weight will allow it to fall to the ground and sink into it, and it must be as shiny and pure and immaculate as it was when it first emerged.

The image on the face of the coin is clearly manifest. It not only shows that the soul is created in God's Image; it proclaims that the soul is that Image, the same Image God possesses within His own pure divine Essence. And here, in this Image, God loves and comprehends Himself and rejoices in Himself. He lives and works and has His Being in the soul.

By this action the soul becomes God-hued, divinized, reformed in the form of God. It possesses everything by grace which God possesses by nature by way of its union with Him and by sinking into Him. Thus the soul soars far above itself, right into the very core of God. So much does the soul take on God's hue that, could it behold itself, it would take itself for God. And whoever would perceive the soul would find it clothed with the divine form, God-hued, by the light of grace; and he would rejoice greatly in it, for in this union God and the soul are one, not by nature but by grace.

The reverse is the case if one could look deeply into the soul and discover how it willfully perverted its love and its ground by taking on the shade of created things. Such a soul would then not appear very different from the devil, who is foul and hideous to behold. If we could see him honestly the way he is, we would run for our lives at that loathsome sight. And this abominable vision the soul will have to endure eternally, should it be found deeply attached to transitory things at the moment of death. Indeed such preoccupations with created things will prove to be as useless and terrifying as the devil himself.

The pure, divine, and liberated soul, however, will be gazed upon eternally in the same manner in which God is contemplated, and so enraptured will it be in this union that it will see itself as God, for God and the soul are one.

Ah, how blissful, how superabundantly full of bliss are those who allow themselves to be sought and found, so that the Lord leads them into His own to such an ineffable union! Nobody can express this adequately, for it far transcends what our senses and our poor human reason can grasp.

Whoever wishes to arrive there, let him choose this path with prudence, then he cannot go astray. However, if he fails to do this and is unable to shed his inordinate attachments, he will necessarily fall behind, now and forever.

May the Lord help us to enter upon this rightful path!

AMEN.

SERMON 39

[FOURTH SUNDAY AFTER TRINITY II]

Estote misericordes sicut et pater vester misericors est
Be merciful, as your Father is merciful (Lk 6:36)

The second interpretation of this Gospel text speaks of four measures which will be given to men, and of the two stages in the divine life; it also speaks of the way in which we ought to love our neighbor.

In this week's Gospel one reads that Our Lord said: "Be merciful, as your Father is merciful: forgive, that you may be forgiven: give, that it may be given to you. You will be measured with the same measure that you measure with; and you will be given good measure, a measure heaped up, a measure pressed down, a measure overflowing."

A word on the first point: "Be merciful, as your Father is merciful." Beloved, this virtue has become very rare nowadays. Each of you is bound to be merciful to his neighbor in all his needs, not only by the giving of gifts, but also by bearing with his weaknesses in a merciful way. But instead, everybody falls upon his neighbor, inflicting poisonous judgments on him. If an unforeseen misfortune befalls him, his neighbor comes running and adds his share to the harm. That way he increases the burden, worsens the blow, and lets it appear in the most depressing light. What untold miseries are the result of malicious talk, which people are always ready to listen to before the facts have been considered. I beg you to at least allow some time for reflection, so that you may know what you are saying. It is a shameful and vicious thing to judge your neighbor in such a way. Our Lord has said: "Judge not, that you may not be judged. For with what judgment you judge, you shall be judged; and with what measure you measure, it shall be measured to you again."

But enough of this. Let us attempt to understand what Our Lord has told us concerning the different kinds of measures. He speaks of four measures which will be given to men: good, heaped up, pressed down, and overflowing, and this is how holy men have interpreted them. The good measure applies to those who live in such a way that it may gain them eternal life. The second, the measure heaped up, applies to their bodies, that they may be glorified with their souls on Judgment Day. The measure pressed down points to the communion of saints, and the measure overflowing, the greatest of all, to our rejoicing in God without any intermediary.

However, we may interpret these "measures" in still another way. First, let us consider this measure, this vessel men measure with; and then who it is who does the measuring. The measure is our capacity to love, which resides in the will. This is indeed the measure with which our work and our life and our eternal happiness are measured; neither more, nor less, but just as much as our measure. And the measurer who metes out this measure is your understanding illumined by grace.

The first thing to note about the good measure is the fact that we must turn our will to God and live according to His mandates and those of Holy Church, receiving the sacraments and holding to the Faith; that we repent our sins and firmly resolve not to sin again; that we live a life of penance as few nowadays do; that we live God-fearing lives and love God and our neighbor.

This, Beloved, is what it means to lead a Christian life and to be a Christian; this is the good measure, the life which leads without doubt to eternal life. And here I should like to make an additional point, namely, that God has invited and called a great number of men to this measure, and more than this He does not demand from them. Indeed, they may have lived lives of such wholeness, according to this way, that they attain eternal life without any stage of purgation.

Yet this is the lowest stage of all the ways that lead to God. There are others who are called by God to a much higher stage, to a higher destination. Nevertheless some of these will have to suffer purgatorial pains of such intensity that no human heart can fathom. However, once they have passed through this, God will raise them a thousand times higher than the others. When a man sets out on a spiritual journey, there is no end to the external exercises he is determined to perform: prostrating himself in prayer, fasting, and many such pious practices. And then he is given a measure heaped up, an inward exercise, when he seeks God with all his strength in the depth of his ground, for there is the Kingdom of God. Beloved, there is so great a difference between these two ways as there is between running and sitting still. If you can reach a stage where your eternal devotions do not impede your interior life, well and good; two things are better than one. But if you find that your external practices interfere with the interior ones, be determined to give them up. You know how we priests observe our Office: In Lent we recite numerous psalms and prayers of different kinds, but when Easter comes, we shorten our regular Office, and for a while we only say three psalms, one antiphon, and a collect. On major feasts, we omit the Office of Our Lady and the petitions.

Each time, then, when God calls you to the great feast of interior contemplation, boldly omit any external practice of piety which hinders it, because your interior life is a divine life, filled with the sweetest delectation. Let your meditation feed on any consideration which induces love: Our Lord's Humanity, His Passion, His sacred wounds, the divine Godhead; the Blessed Trinity, God's omnipotence, wisdom, and mercy, or all His goodness toward yourself. Whatever it is that most inspires you, give thanks for it, and let it carry you into the depth of the soul, into its inmost ground, and there await your God. Such an exercise, performed with love, enables us to receive God far more than external devotions ever could. The more inward a devotion is, the better it is: for the external always derives its power from the internal. Just as one drop of a potent wine can change an entire cartload of water into a noble wine, so one drop of your interior life enables and exalts your external devotions.

Now, there are some people who have vessels which are extremely wide; they know how to meditate in a spiritual way, but their vessels are barely an inch deep, because they are lacking humility and universal charity. Saint Augustine said: "What matters is not the time spent in prayer or the amount of good works, but the greatness of your love." Look at the men who reap the corn and gather the grapes: They are not the ones who feast on it; rough bread and water is their fare.

Next comes the measure heaped up and pressed down; this is the outpouring love which attracts everything to itself: all good works, all vitality, all suffering, it draws all into its vessel: everything good that is done in the world, be it done by good men or by evil.

For, if your love is greater than the love of those who perform good works, then, because of the greatness of your love, their good works become more yours than theirs. How many psalms and vigils are recited, how many Masses are said and sung, how many works of self-denial are performed which do not profit those who perform them, but those who have the fullness of this love. They are the ones who receive everything into their measure! Nothing in the whole world can elude them; but God is not mindful of those who do not intend Him in their works. Hence Saint Paul says: "Even if I give all I possess to the poor, even if I let them burn my body, if I have not love I am still nothing."

Everything depends on love. The evil that we do remains our own, but the good that we do is attributed to love, just as the grain that is poured into a measure rushes in and is pressed together, as if it all wanted to become one single grain. Love attracts all the good there is in heaven, in all the Angels and the saints and all the sufferings of the martyrs; and furthermore, love draws to itself all the good that is contained in all creatures in heaven and on earth, of which so much is lost, or at least seems to be lost. It is love that keeps it from perishing. The spiritual masters and the saints tell us that eternal life is filled with a love that is exceedingly great; when one soul recognizes that another possesses a greater love than it has itself, it rejoices as much as if it were its own. And the closer we come to such a disposition on earth, the more glorious will be our joy in eternity.

Now, he whose measure contains the most love here on earth will receive the greatest joy in Heaven. The devil hates to see this, and he tempts us to self-righteousness and to thinking of our neighbor and his works as inferior to our own. Thus we deprive ourselves of love by judging others and by deprecating their works; the result is that our words turn into arrows of deadly poison shot from a bow. And what is the target of these arrows? It is our own souls, which they pierce with the wounds of everlasting death, and everything we had stored up in our measure is now spilt and lost. A more terrifying and distressing process cannot be imagined.

So, guard your tongues! Or the devil will come and imbue your heart with an aversion against some good person and make you pass malicious judgment upon him; and you will give expression to this aversion. Immediately, you lose the share you have up to then possessed in this man's graces, his acts of virtue, and most of all in the innermost core of his love. Of this share the Prophet has spoken when he said that the oil of consecration flowed down from the head of Aaron upon his beard. This beard has many hairs, but they all make up one beard, so that they all receive the benignant oil that flows into it. That hair, however, that would separate itself from the whole, be it ever so small, would receive not a single drop of the precious chrism. The same is true of love. As long as it is all-encompassing, as long as it shares its graces without making distinctions, it will remain the precious and mellifluous chrism of all good; but as soon as you exclude anyone or anything from your love, you receive nothing of this oil.

Beloved, take very good care that your love embraces everyone. Show charity toward all and deprive no one of his peace! Do not destroy the temple which the great High Priest has consecrated within you, and do not bring down God's judgment upon you. Alas, human nature has become alienated from brotherly love. If a man sees his brother fall, it may perhaps cause him some grief; but there he stands and lets it be, so perverted has his love become. Beware of your failings, see if your love is perfect, and learn to fear the Lord as long as you are on this earth; once you have left it, it will be too late. There will be no chance to do or undo anything; then, even if the Mother of God and all the saints interceded for us with tears of blood, it would be of no avail. So be on your guard now! God is constantly waiting for us, eager to bestow new graces; what we miss now we shall never receive. True love never fails. Saint Paul says: "Love never wearies, love does everything, suffers everything." Such is the love of the men I have been speaking to you about.

And now we come to the measure overflowing, the measure which is so full, so rich and abundant, that it overflows on every side. Our Lord touches this measure with but one finger, and at once it overflows with the riches of God's gifts far beyond anything it had ever contained. Everything pours out of the measure and flows back to the Source from which it originated, straight back to it, to lose itself there completely. All wanting, all knowing, all loving, all understanding has overflowed and is lost in God and one with Him. God sees Himself in such souls and He loves; whatever they do, it is His work in them. And this overflowing knows no limit, so strong is the urge of such souls to pour their love out to others. Oh, dear Lord, they say, "take pity on those sinners who have performed good works but have fallen short in the end. Give them the crumbs that have fallen from your rich table, and let them find salvation through the cleansing fire of purgatory!"

"Oh, dear Lord, give them your crumbs!" And thus their measure overflows into the entire Church, into saints and sinners, carrying everything back into the ground of the Godhead, every good that has ever been achieved. No work is ever wasted, from the smallest to the greatest: not the briefest prayer, not a single good intention, not the smallest act of faith. In this active love they offer to Him, their Heavenly Father, all this and all that the Angels and saints in Heaven possess: for this overflowing measure contains even the love and beatitude of the Blessed. Beloved, if it were not for such men, the rest of us would be in a bad way.

Let us pray to Our Lord that we, too, may achieve this overflowing measure.

AMEN.

SERMON 40

[FIFTH SUNDAY AFTER TRINITY I]

Carissimi, estote unanimes in oratione
Beloved, be you all of one mind in prayer (1 Pt 3:8)

This Sermon takes its text from the Epistle for the Fifth
Sunday after Trinity and demonstrates the three stages in
the spiritual life. It instructs us to strive upward with all
our might, to pray in spirit, and to raise our entire activity
to a divine level.

In this Sunday's Epistle Saint Peter exhorts us to be single-minded
in prayer,* and here he touches upon the most profitable, pleasing, and noble work we can perform. It is an act so fruitful and so
rich in love that no other act on earth can surpass it.

Listen now to what I want to tell you about the nature of prayer,
its essence and method, and in what place we ought to pray.

What is prayer? Its essence, so the saints and spiritual masters
tell us, is an ascent of mind and heart to God. It is the Lord Himself
who teaches us that the place in which we ought to pray is in the
spirit.

Now I would like to talk briefly about the nature and method
of prayer, how one should enter upon it, and how one should be disposed. Every good man who wishes to pray should first begin with
recollection, bring his senses to a focus in himself, and be sure that
his spirit is totally turned toward God. In this recollection there are
three stages: a highest, a lowest, and a middle one. It is also advisable
that each of us should examine carefully what it is that launches his

---

*The single-mindedness of the praying soul serves as leitmotiv for Tauler's sermon.
The sense is not that of Saint Peter's Epistle passage (1 Pt 3:8) as it is traditionally rendered.

136

soul most swiftly and what may touch off real and true devotion most effectively, and then put this particular method into practice. One thing, however, is certain: If we work to achieve genuine and effective prayer, if we wish to be truly heard, then we must turn our back upon transitory and external matters, on all that is not of God, be it friends or strangers. Also we must turn away from all kinds of frivolity, fashion, adornments, jewels, or anything else that is not truly rooted in God. And furthermore we must keep our speech disciplined and our conduct blameless, protecting both from any disorder, from without or within.

This is how we ought to prepare ourselves for true prayer. When Saint Peter says that we should be single-minded, he means that we should cling to God as our sole and supreme good, that at the moment of prayer we must fix our soul's gaze firmly and unswervingly on Him, and adhere to God with patience and love.

Beloved, everything we call our own surely comes from God. The least we can do is to refer back to Him what we have received, keeping mind and heart firmly fixed on Him, unscattered and single-minded. And then we must bring to a focus all our strength of mind and spirit and raise them up to God.

This is the proper manner in which to pray. Never believe that true prayer consists in mere babbling, reciting so many psalms and vigils, saying your beads while you allow your thoughts to roam. If you notice that such practices of devotion, however great and good they may seem, get in the way of the prayer in spirit, give them up without hesitation. This does not apply to the Divine Office, which you are obliged to say by the precepts of the Church; but with this exception be quite determined to drop everything that presents an obstacle to the prayer of the spirit.

Now it happens sometimes that a whole community is obligated to undertake long and formal prayers of petition for some special intention. How should a spiritual-minded person act when he feels hindered by vocal and external prayers? Well, he ought to say them and at the same time not say them. But how should he do this? He should recollect himself in the central point of his soul and raise his heart to God with great might, inwardly gazing upon God's presence, and ardently longing for whatever is dearest to God's will. He should die to self and to all created things and immerse himself ever deeper in God's most holy will. And then he should draw into his prayer all things that have been commended to him, intending only the honor and glory of God to the profit and consolation of all those for whom he is asked to pray. That way he will have prayed far better than if he had recited the prayer of a thousand people.

This prayer in spirit vastly surpasses all external prayer. It is the prayer our Heavenly Father wants us to say, and all other kinds exist only to that end. And if they do not lead you to it, do not be afraid to give them up. The whole process can be likened to the building of a cathedral; all kinds of work is going on, with perhaps a hundred workmen laboring or contributing in other ways. Some carry stones, others mix the mortar, everywhere there is activity, but it is all directed to one end, which is the building and finishing of the cathedral. The efforts are intended to build God's House, which is a House of Prayer. And hence all the work is undertaken for the sake of prayer, prayer being the purpose all these various activities serve. And so it is with inward spiritual prayer: The work that has helped toward its achievement has been well spent when it reaches its proper end. Such prayer is far superior to the external kind, unless we are so well practiced that the two could be joined without effort, one never impeding the other. Then the enjoyment and activity would be one, as they are in God, where the very highest activity and the very purest enjoyment form a single unity: utmost fulfillment without hindrance, with activity residing in the divine Persons, enjoyment in the simple ground of the divine Essence.

The Heavenly Father, in His divine attribute of Fatherhood, is pure activity. Everything in Him is activity, for it is by the act of self-comprehension that He begets His beloved Son, and both in an ineffable embrace breathe forth the Holy Spirit. Their mutual love is an eternal, essential activity of the Persons, and yet they rest in themselves in the uncreated being and simplicity of the divine Essence. And here there is a silent, simple enjoying, a simple consuming of God's being, and activity and enjoyment are one. Now since God has made His creatures in His likeness, activity is inherent in all of them. The firmament, the sun and stars, and far above them Angels and men—all are active in their proper way. There is no flower so small, no blade of grass so tiny, that the heavenly bodies did not work in them. And, above all, God Himself is at work in them. Is it surprising, then, that man, that noble creature, fashioned in God's Image, should resemble Him in His activity? Since he is endowed with faculties in God's Image, ought he not be like Him in being? This noble creature must act with far greater nobility than created things, such as the heavens, which are devoid of reason. The whole of creation should follow man because of his likeness to God both in action and in contemplation. No matter in what direction man turns with his higher and lower faculties, he is forever active; and each of his faculties acts in a way commensurate to its object. Be it God or some created thing, man's faculties act upon an object according to its nature.

Now, whoever makes God and heavenly things the object of his activity, leaving temporal concerns far behind, his works would indeed become divinized. The noble, dearest soul of Our Lord Jesus Christ was in its highest faculties unceasingly turned toward the Godhead; from His first day on earth, His soul was directed toward that goal. His soul then possessed the same beatific knowledge of the Father as He does now. In the lower faculties He was active, moving and suffering, for, in Our Lord's earthly life, joy, work, and sorrow were joined. Even when He hung dying upon the Cross, He possessed in His highest faculties the same joy in God's presence as He does now in Heaven. And all those of us who would faithfully follow Him in our surrender to what is divine, in whom activity and joyful contemplation have become one, they will resemble Him closest after death, when their whole being will be rapt in essential and eternal joy.

Beloved, those who neglect this noble work and let their noble faculties lie idle thwart themselves in a grave and terrifying way. They live in a most distressing manner. By wasting precious time, they incur countless and intolerable pains in purgatory, and their eternal reward will be small. They will resemble an uncouth peasant, unfit to appear at court and to render personal service to the King in His inner chamber. Indeed, in eternity these vain worldlings will be considered a thousand times less fit than an uncouth peasant to come into God's presence, where His beloved friends will dwell with Him in eternity. Those idlers who live without God both in thought and in action are plainly inciting the evil spirits to tempt them, and lay themselves open to attack.

We have said before that man's likeness to God lies in his capacity to act and enjoy simultaneously. This means that inwardly he can immutably adhere to God in a profound, perfect, and pure desire. Such a state differs as greatly from the outward manner of serving God as do running and sitting down. The state we are speaking of is an awareness of God's presence, an inward, contemplative desire. In its inward aspect it is a joyful contemplation; in its outward aspect it is directed toward activity to the benefit and good of all. Yet this movement away from inwardness happens only for the sake of the return. In this the interior life is always the guardian of the exterior, just as a master workman who has many young apprentices and servants under him; they all work according to his instructions. He, however, does not work among them; he appears rarely and then only to supervise their work. He quickly lays out the rules and does the planning, and they proceed accordingly, and yet one attributes the work to him, because of his instructions and skill, as if he alone had done it all. And everything is called his because he masterminded it. Therefore it is more his work than the work of those who have carried it out.

The same is true of an inward, regenerate person; his enjoyment is all inward. With the light of reason he swiftly surveys his exterior faculties and instructs them in their activity; but inwardly he is immersed and drawn into God, joyfully adhering to Him. And in this state he remains unhindered by his activity. Yet all his exterior works serve only the interior one—there is no work so small that it would not be tributary to it. And thus we may see that all the various activities comprise one single good work.

The same order exists in Holy Church, which we call corpus mysticum, the Mystical Body of which Christ is the Head. It exists in our physical body, which also has many members: There is the eye, which sees the whole body, but not itself; the mouth, which eats and drinks for the sake of the whole body, not only for itself; the hand, the foot, and the various members all have their particular function to perform, and all the functions serve the whole body under one head. In the same manner, there is no work in the whole of Christendom so small and insignificant—be it the ringing of the bells or the lighting of a candle—that it does not serve the perfection of this interior work.

Beloved, the harmony within the Mystical Body must be as complete as that between the members of our phsyical body; no member must exist apart from this solidarity, causing harm or injury to another; it must see itself in all, for the gain of one is the common gain of all. And should we know a member within the Mystical Body worthier than we are, then we should hold it dearer than we hold ourselves. The arm or the hand takes more care of the head, the heart, or the eyes than it does of itself; and so must God's members be animated by an impulsive love for our neighbor, which increases the more he is loved by Christ, our Head. And whatever good Our Lord wished to give him would be the same as if it were mine. If I love the good in him more than he does himself, then it is more mine than his. The evil which he does is his own. The good which I love in him is truly mine.

That Saint Paul was rapt in ecstasy was granted by God to him, not to me. But if I savor [in this event] God's will, then I had rather that this ecstasy were his than mine, and by my loving it in him, it becomes truly mine. This should be my attitude toward every living person, even if he were on the other side of the ocean, even if he were my enemy. Such is the harmony that reigns in the Mystical Body. And thus I would be endowed with all the riches of heaven and earth which God's lovers possess in union with the Head of that Body. Everything which they and He possess together, all the riches of Heaven and earth, of the Angels and the saints, must really and truly flow into me, if only I am formed according to God's will to be a member subject to the Head, united to Him in love with all his members, and so sculptured into His likeness as to be lifted out of my own self.

Here it becomes quite clear whether we love God and His will more than we love ourselves and our own will. Not all that glitters is gold; indeed, if tested, it frequently turns out to be less than copper. Those, however, who have denied themselves and forsaken all are truly poor in spirit, even if they possessed the whole world. Beloved, such constancy in love, such sharing in joy and sorrow, is rarely found anywhere in the world.

It is time now to speak of the three stages [in the mystical life], a lowest, a middle, and a highest stage. The first stage, a life of spirituality and virtue, brings us close to God's presence, and in order to attain this, we must turn completely to the wonderful works of God and to the manifestations of the ineffable gifts which overflow from God's hidden goodness. From this derives a state of soul named "jubilatio." The second stage is spiritual poverty, when in a strange manner God withdraws Himself from the soul, leaving it anguished and denuded. The third stage is the transition into a divinized life, into a union of our created spirit with God's uncreated one. This we may call a true transformation of the whole being, and it is hard to believe that those who achieve such a stage could ever fall away from God.

JOHANNES TAULER

We attain the first stage, that of jubilation, by reflecting on the wondrous tokens of love which God has so marvelously granted to us in Heaven and on earth; the abundance of favors God has shown to us and to all His creatures; how all nature—verdant and blossoming—is filled with His glory; how He has flooded the whole of creation with His unfathomable mercy; and the great gifts He gave to man, how He has sought him out, guided and enriched him; how He invited and taught him and watched over him with patience; how, for our sake He has become man, suffered, and offered His life and soul for us in order to draw us closer to Him than words can express; and how the Most Blessed Trinity has awaited us to share in its eternal joy. When we reflect on all this with profound love, a great and active joy will be born in us. And whoever reflects on these matters lovingly will be overwhelmed by such interior joy that his feeble body cannot contain it, and it results in a special outburst of joy. Were it not for this outward expression, strange phenomena would occur, such as physical disorders. Thus it is granted to man to taste how sweet the Lord is, and he experiences union with God in a spiritual embrace. So God attracts, invites, and draws man out of himself, from a state of unlikeness into one of likeness.

Let no one attempt to interfere with these children of God or impose outward observances and activities on them. By distracting them thus, they would only destroy themselves. There is no need for the Prior to know where a brother has gone when he leaves the choir after the Divine Office; only a useless religious needs such supervision. One day Our Lord offered to one He loved very dearly His divine kiss. But he answered and said: "Lord, this is not what I want at all. If I were taken out of myself with joy, it would be of no use to you. How could I then pray for the poor souls and help them out of purgatory? And how could I pray for poor sinners?" The sinners and poor souls cannot help themselves. It is up to us who are still on earth to hasten to their aid. God wills us to offer our help because His justice must be perfectly satisfied. And that is the obligation of all lovers of God who are still on earth. What great love that man possessed, renouncing such sweet and great comfort from such a motive!

Now for the second stage: When God has drawn a man far away from created things and made him grow from childhood to maturity, when God has fortified him with spiritual sweetness, then he is offered coarser food; for he now is a man and has become of age. For a grown man, a strong diet is wholesome and good; he no longer needs milk and soft bread. An extremely rough path lies ahead of him, dark and lonely, and as he is led through it, God deprives him of everything He had given him before. The man is now left so completely on his own that he knows nothing at all of God; he is brought to such desolation that he wonders whether he was ever on the right path, whether he has a God or not, whether he really exists; he is so strangely afflicted, so deeply afflicted, that he feels that the whole wide world has become too narrow for him. He can neither taste God nor know Him, and since everything else is insufficient, he feels himself hemmed in between two walls with a sword behind him and a sharp spear in front. What is he to do? Both ways are blocked. Let him sit down and say: "Welcome, bitter affliction, full of grace!" To love and to be denied the object of one's love surely would seem worse than any hell, if there could be one on earth. Whatever one could say to such a man would be of no more comfort than a stone. One cannot speak to him of God, and even less of creatures. The stronger his experience of God was before, the stronger and more intolerable is now the bitterness and pain of loss.

But be of good cheer. The Lord is not far away. Cling to the rock of the true and living faith. Your anguish will soon be over, though in this state your poor soul cannot conceive that this insufferable darkness could ever give way to light.

For when our Lord has prepared a man's soul by such intolerable trials—and they are a better preparation than any pious devotion—He then comes and raises the soul to the highest stage. And here Our Lord gives him new eyes to see and reveals to him the truth. Now the sun rises in bright splendor and lifts the soul above all its former afflictions. Such a person has indeed returned from death to life. He is led out of himself and enters into Him, the Lord. And now God compensates him for all his anguish and heals him of all his wounds. He raises him from a human to a divine mode of being, from sorrow into a divine peace, in which man becomes so divinized that everything which he is and does, God is and does in him. Such a person is raised so far above any natural mode that he truly becomes by grace what God is essentially by nature. In this state, man feels himself lost in God. He neither knows nor feels nor experiences his former self; he knows only God's simple essence.

Beloved, to have attained this state is truly to have reached the deepest depth of humility, for in this state we have been brought to nothing. It surpasses our powers of comprehension, for here we have reached the most perfect knowledge of our own nothingness. Deeper than this we cannot penetrate into the depth of humility, and the deeper we sink, the higher we rise, for height and depth are here identical. And if a man were to fall from such a height back again upon himself, relapsing into human pride, such a fall would be like the fall of Lucifer.

This is the state at which he attains the true single-mindedness in prayer of which today's Epistle speaks: that we should become one with God.

May God grant us all to achieve it.

AMEN.

SERMON 44
[FEAST OF THE NATIVITY OF JOHN THE BAPTIST II]

Hic venit ut testimonium perhiberat de lumine
He came to bear witness to the light (Jn 1:7)

The second Sermon on John the Baptist speaks of two kinds of light: the light of grace and the light of glory. It tells us in what manner we should receive the witness, so that we may experience sweet love, agonizing love, and enraptured love.

"He came to bear witness to the light." This week our mother, Holy Church, celebrates the Feast of the Nativity of the great and honorable Saint John the Baptist. There is little we can contribute with our praise, since his honor and greatness were praised by Our Lord Jesus Christ Himself, Who said no one born of woman has been of such greatness as he.

Our Lord also said: "What did you go to see? A prophet? This man is greater than a prophet. What did you go out for? To see a man clothed in soft garments? Or a reed shaken to and fro by the wind? No, there is nothing of the kind here." John said of himself that he was a voice crying in the wilderness: "Prepare the way of the Lord, make straight His path." Also, in our Office we sing this week that he was a burning and a shining lantern. John the Evangelist referred to him as a witness to the light. It is about these last words that I want to talk to you today.

Is there any higher praise we could give to this saint? He is called "a witness to the light." This light of which he was a witness was a real light, transcendent, beyond all our comprehension. This light illuminates the innermost core, the deepest ground of the soul. And when this light and this witness is brought to bear on us, instead of receiving it where it shines we turn away from the depth of our soul and run in the opposite direction, turning everything the wrong way around. We fail to receive the witness because we are so immersed in external activities. There are others, too, who will not accept the light because they are opposed to it. "He came to His own," says the Evangelist, "and His own received Him not." These are the people with worldly dispositions, resembling the Pharisees, whom Saint John called descendants of vipers, though they called themselves descendants of Abraham. They stand in opposition to all who love the light, and they are in a most grievous and precarious state. They cling to the light of the Faith by a single thread.

Now, we must bear in mind that human nature is weak and seriously flawed. That is why our merciful God has come to its rescue with supernatural aid and supernatural power. This is the light of grace. It is a created light, but it lifts nature high above itself and brings with it all the nourishment which it will require for a new life. Beyond that there is an uncreated light, the light of glory, which is God Himself. If we ever are to know God, it must be through Him, with Him, and in Him: God through God; as the Prophet says: "Lord in Your light we shall see the light." This is an overflowing light, enlightening every man who comes into the world. It shines upon everyone, the bad as well as the good, just as the sun shines upon all creatures. If they are blind to it, so much the worse for them. If a man finds himself in a darkened house, he needs only sufficient light to find a window. Then he can open it and put his head out and he is in the light. Such a man becomes a witness to the light.

Now let us see how we should act initially, when we are about to receive this witness. We must detach ourselves from everything that is temporal and transitory, for this witness is to be received by the lower and higher faculties within us. The lowest faculty is our appetite for pleasure and the irascible appetite. Hence it is the faculty for pleasure which will first receive this witness, and therefore we must cut ourselves off from all those natural pleasures we find most gratifying: society, fashion, in short anything which satisfies the senses, though God permits us to satisfy our needs. It is indeed a wilderness into which God is taking us: a life of detachment in which we shed our desires, spiritual and natural, in our interior and exterior life.

Secondly, this witness comes to our irascible appetite, teaching us perseverance and strength. When we have received this testimony, we become immovable, like an iron mountain, instead of being swayed to and fro like a reed. When Our Lord said of Saint John that he was not clothed in soft garments, he was alluding to people who seek bodily pleasures for their comfort. But there are many who despise those, and yet are like reeds. They are moved by what people say; a sarcastic or severe word can throw them completely off balance. How foolish! What harm can such words do? Then along comes the devil with his insinuating voices, making them feel now high and then low. They are indeed reeds shaken by the wind.

But this testimony is given to our higher faculties as well: to our reason, will, and love. In our reason, it is a prophet; prophet means "one who sees far, *videns.*" Reason is far-seeing, it amazes one how far it sees. If an enlightened man who had not yet attained this degree were to hear things mysterious to him, his reason would bear witness in the depths of his soul and say: "Yes, this is true." But Our Lord said: "He is more than a prophet." That is, in this depth, which reason cannot penetrate, we behold light within light. We now move within this inward light, the light of grace: and thus we behold and perceive, by means of the created light, the divine, uncreated One.

All this comes to us first in a veiled manner, for our faculties cannot come within a thousand miles of this depth of the soul. The breadth which opens up here has neither form nor image nor any other mode or manner; nor are there any concepts of space. For it is an unfathomable abyss, poised in itself, unplumbed, ebbing and flowing like the sea. As one is immersed in it, it seems still and void; yet in an instant it wells up as if it would engulf all things. One sinks into this abyss, and in it is God's own dwelling-place, more real than in Heaven and in all His creatures. Whoever finds his way there would truly find God, and himself one with God, for God would never part from it again. God would be present to him, and here eternity would be tasted and savored, for there exists no past or future.

No created light can touch this ground and illumine it, for it is truly God's home and dwelling-place. The whole of creation would not fill or plumb this void, nothing created could ever penetrate it or fulfill its yearnings. God alone can fill it with His divine immensity.

This abyss of the soul belongs to the divine abyss, to nothing less. As it is said: "Deep calls on deep." And if we are carefully attentive, this ground sheds light upon our faculties, drawing and leading the higher and lower ones back to their source and their origin. If only we would adhere closely to this depth, we would perceive the lovely, divine accents of that voice which calls us into the wilderness, into the ground, drawing us ever deeper.

No one can imagine the solitude which reigns in this wilderness, no one at all. No thought can enter here, not a word of all the learned treatises on the Holy Trinity with which people busy themselves so much. Not a single word. So inward is it, so infinitely remote, and so untouched by time and space. This ground is simple and without differentiation, and when one enters here, it will seem as if one has been here from all eternity, and as if united to God, be it only for an instant. This experience sheds light and bears witness that man was everlasting in God, before his creation in time. When he was in Him, he was God in God.

Saint John writes: "Everything that has been made was one life in Him." What man now is in his createdness, he was from the beginning in God's uncreatedness, one with Him in essence. And until he returns to that imageless state which was his when he issued from the origin, from uncreatedness to createdness, he will never find his way back into God. Every natural inclination, every adherence to creatures, every trace of complacency must be left far behind. And along with it, all possessiveness which may stain the depth of the soul, all the inordinate pleasures of soul or body freely consented to, they all must vanish. Unless they are utterly eradicated, unless man is as he was when he first emerged from God, he will never attain to the Source.

Nor is this liberation from human images and forms sufficient: Our human spirit must first be clothed with the divine form by the light of grace. If we give ourselves to this reforming in the form of God, if we withdraw into this ground and remain there in perfect order, we might well be granted in the present life a glimpse of this divine transformation, although no one can enter into God or comprehend Him except in the uncreated light which is God Himself: "*Domine, in lumine tuo videbimus lumen.*" A person who often turns to this inmost ground and is at home there will be granted many a lofty glimpse, though of brief duration. He will then behold God clearer and more distinctly than he can behold the sun with his bodily eyes.

This ground of the soul was already known by the pagan philosophers. As they searched its depth, the knowledge of it caused them to think poorly of transitory things. Such great masters as Proclus and Plato gave a lucid account of it, in order to guide those who could not find the way by themselves. Saint Augustine says that Plato had already fully foreseen the first part of Saint John's Gospel, "In the beginning was the Word" up to "there was a man sent from God." The expression of this knowledge was still inchoate, although the Holy Trinity was already prefigured in their thought. This understanding, my Beloved, arose from their inmost ground, for which they lived and which they cherished.

Is it not shameful and a great scandal that we poor latecomers, we Christians, aided by grace, the Faith, and the sacraments, should be running about like blind hens, ignorant of our own self and of the depth within us? The reason is that we are so fragmented, so scattered all over the lot. We put great emphasis on what appeals to the senses, on our activities and various projects. The number of vigils and psalms and other pious practices occupy us to such an extent that we cannot find the way to our inmost ground.

My dear Sisters, if we cannot fill our casks with the noble wine of Cyprus, then let us fill them with stones and ashes, so as not to provide space for the devil by leaving them entirely empty. This would be preferable to reeling off one's beads in a mindless manner.

There is still another witness in our higher faculties; it is in the faculty which enables us to love and to will. We have sung about it this week: "*Lucerna lucens et ardens,*" a shining and burning lantern. This lantern gives light and heat. Your hand can feel the heat, but you cannot see the flame unless you look down on it, where you can see the light glimmering through the panes. If you only paid attention to this comparison, you would be more receptive to its light and heat! It is the wounding love which will lead you into this ground. And as long as you feel it within yourself, it must drive you on, so that you can bend the bow to the utmost in order to hit the supreme target.

But once you have come into that hidden abyss, into captive love, you must let love have its way. No longer do you have any command over yourself, over your thoughts, your practices, or even your works of virtue. If, when in this state, you are left enough liberty and space for thought, you will fall back again into wounding love. But if this happens, summon all your strength, raise yourself up, storm ahead with your love, compel it to rush forward aided by all the desire and prayer you are capable of. Even if you cannot speak, let your desires and thoughts speak, as Saint Augustine said: "Lord, you have ordained that I should love you; grant what you have ordained. You have ordained that I should love you with all my heart, with all my soul, with all my strength, with all my spirit. Grant me, O Lord, that I may love you above all else." And if you cannot conceptualize all this at the moment, say it out aloud. Do not be like the people who just sit and wait: They will never experience that love.

After this comes agonizing love, and finally, in the fourth place, enraptured love. Alas, my dear Sisters, how much has this love decreased nowadays, and how much has natural reason increased! People have never used their reason more cunningly than when it comes to buying and selling. Enraptured love can be compared to our lantern. Whoever loves with this love knows its heat. It makes him impetuous in all his faculties; he longs and yearns for this love, not knowing that he possesses it. It consumes his very flesh and blood. Now is the moment to do yourself harm with external practices and devotions. If love is to do its work, you must do nothing to withdraw from it, but follow it through all its tempests. There are some who want to take shelter from this storm for fear of perishing, saying it is not for them. My beloved! When enraptured love comes upon us, all merely human activities must give way. It is Our Lord Himself who comes and speaks through us: He speaks one Word that is nobler and more telling than are a hundred thousand spoken by men.

Saint Dionysius said: "When the Eternal Word is uttered in the ground of the soul, and the ground is so prepared that it can receive that Word in its unutterable immensity and fruitfulness, not in part but fully, the ground and the Word become one." The ground becomes one with the Word not in essence, for the soul retains its created nature in this union. Our Lord bore witness to this when He said: "Father, let them be one as We are one"; and again when He said to Augustine: "You must be changed into me." No one can attain this stage except through this degree of love. When Saint John the Baptist said: "I am the voice of one crying in the wilderness, make straight the way of the Lord," he refers to the path of the virtues. This path is very straight. And again he says that he is to prepare the Lord's paths. Footpaths reach the goal faster than public roads. The shortcut across the fields is indeed rougher and may lead one astray; and yet it is more direct than the open road.

Beloved! Whoever would discover the paths leading to the ground, he would take the shortest and most direct way, keeping all his energies to himself so as to be very attentive. For these paths are rugged, dark, and alien to our nature, and only those who are sufficiently skilled can take them. If they are aware of this, they will not be put off by hurdles and hindrances or any other human anguish. Quite the opposite: Everything will point to the ground, beckon, and draw them there.

In the same manner we should straighten the paths within ourselves, the paths which lead our spirit to God, and God to us. These relations also require skill, and their difficulties are of a hidden nature. At this point many give up and begin to run after exterior devotions and activities. They are like people starting for Rome and taking the road to Holland. The more they advance, the farther they get away from their destination. And when they return, they are old and spent and no longer up to the tempestuous work of love.

Beloved, when we find ourselves in the tempests of love, we should not dwell on our sins and failings. Our only concern should be that love's work be accomplished. We can be overcome by this tempest even when our hearts appear cold, disinterested and hard. Now more than ever we must adhere to love, clinging to it in perfect faith, freed and stripped of everything that is not love. Constantly long for it, put your whole trust in it, cleave to it, and your experience will be as powerful and overwhelming as is possible in this life. If your faith in love is imperfect, your desire will fade away. Love will be extinguished, and nothing will come of it all.

This may seem very hard to you. The devil will allow you all the marks of a spiritual life, but he will do everything in his power to deprive you of love's true witness. He will leave you with all kinds of treacherous love which many will mistake for the real thing. If they looked deeply into their ground, they would see whether their love was true or false. The one thing necessary is to have access to the ground in order to be able to enter its depth. There you would find that grace which would incessantly raise you up. But man often resists that voice until he makes himself unworthy to ever receive it again. This is due to complacency. If only he would respond to the glance of grace, it would lead him to find such union with God that he would experience in time the joy that will be his in eternity, as some have done before him.

May God grant that we may all experience this.

AMEN.

SERMON 47

[TENTH SUNDAY AFTER TRINITY]

Divisiones ministrationum sunt, idem autem spiritus . . .
There are different kinds of gifts, though it is the same
Spirit . . . (1 Cor 12:6)

This Sermon, preached on the tenth Sunday after Trinity,
is based on the Epistle of Saint Paul in which he urges us
to be mindful of the vocation to which we have been called
by God. We are also admonished to perform works of charity, to exercise all the virtues, and to renounce self-will.

Saint Paul says in today's Epistle: "There are different kinds of
gifts, though it is the same Spirit who is imparted to each man
to make the best advantage of it." It is one and the same Spirit who
works equally in all things. We all receive a revelation so that we may
use it to our best profit and advantage. To one is given the gift of
knowledge, that he may expound the Faith, through the same Spirit
who works differently in someone else. Saint Paul lists a great number of gifts, which are all the work of one and the same Spirit, and
on the whole he mentions those which bear witness to the Faith.

In times past the Holy Spirit worked wondrous things in those
who loved Him in testimony to the Faith; great signs and manifold
prophecies came to pass. There is less need of these today. Know,
however, that nowadays there is less genuine Faith alive among
Christians than there is among pagans and Jews.

Let us now consider the words of Saint Paul: "There are different kinds of gifts though it is the same Spirit who performs them."
Beloved, you can observe in the natural order that the body has
many different parts and senses, and how each particular part,
whether it is eye, ear, mouth, hand, or foot, has its own special func-

tions, its own work to perform. There can be no question of one wanting to perform the work of the other, or to be anything other than what God has meant it to be. Now, we too are all one body and Christ is its Head. In this body the parts are very different from one another. One of us is an eye, another is a hand, someone else is a foot, a mouth, or an ear. The eyes in the body of Holy Christendom are the spiritual masters; that is something you need not concern yourselves with. But we ordinary Christians ought to examine carefully what is our work to which Our Lord has called and invited us, and what the grace is the Lord has granted us, because every service or activity, however insignificant, is a grace, and it is the same Spirit which produces them all for the use and profit of mankind.

Let us start with the humblest task: One person knows how to spin, another how to make shoes; some people are good at practical things, which they perform to best advantage; others are not. All these graces are God-given, the work of His Spirit.

Believe me, if I were not a priest and a religious, I should be very proud to make shoes, and I should try to make them as best as I can, and I should be glad to earn my living with my own hands.

Beloved, foot or hand must not want to be an eye. Everyone ought to do that work to which God has called Him, no matter how modest. Thus each of our Sisters has her own work entrusted to her. Some of them can sing beautifully, and they are responsible for the Divine Office. This is all the work of God's Spirit. Saint Augustine said: "God is unvarying, divine and simple, and yet works in all things in diverse ways. He is one in all, and all in one." There is no task so small, so insignificant or menial, that it is not a proof of God's special grace. Everyone should do for his neighbor what his neighbor cannot do as well for himself, and that way, by his love, grace gives way to grace. You may be sure of this: If we are not giving and helpful to our neighbor, we shall have to account for it before God, for as the Gospel tells us, everyone will have to give an account of his stewardship. Each one of us must return to our brothers as best as he can what he has received from God.

Why is it, then, there is so much grumbling, everyone complaining that his work stands in the way of his sanctification? It is God who gave him his work, and God never put a hindrance in our way. Why are people so discontented and dissatisfied? Is not all work imparted to man by God's Spirit? And yet we do not see it that way and we remain disappointed. You must know that it is not the work that causes your trouble but the disordered way in which you go about it. If you did your work, as you easily could, and as you certainly should, meaning God alone and not yourself, you would not be anxious to please or afraid to displease anyone; you would not be asking for your own profit or pleasure, because you would seek God's glory alone in all your activities. If you looked at it that way, neither reproach nor scruples could trouble you. Any spiritual person ought to be ashamed of doing his work in such a disordered way, and with so little purity of intention, that it openly causes him anxiety. This only shows that the works were not done in God nor were they caused by genuine and pure love for God and for the benefit of his neighbor. If you remain content in your work it will be a proof, to you and to others, that you have been keeping your eye on God alone.

When Our Lord reproved Martha, it was not because of her work—it was good and holy—but because she was overly concerned.

We must perform good and useful work, in whatever way it comes to us; the care, however, should be left to God. We ought to do our work meticulously, silently, and with inward recollection. With such a disposition we shall draw God into it, for the eyes of our soul will be turned inward, devoutly and lovingly. And always we should examine our motives and rectify our intentions. We must listen to the Holy Spirit, whether He prompts us to rest or to work, and then be faithful to His promptings. If He wishes us to rest, let us rest; if He wishes us to work, then let us do it with good cheer. When we come across the old and sick and infirm, let us anticipate their needs and rush to their aid; we should vie with one another for the privilege to perform a work of love, always bearing the other's burdens. You may be sure that if you fail to do this, God will take the task away from you and give it to someone else who will do it promptly, and you will be left useless and empty of virtue and grace. And if while you are at work you feel God's hidden touch, give it all your attention without neglecting your work. Learn to draw God into your activities and do not remove yourself from His touch.

This, my Beloved, is the way to practice the virtues. For practice we must, if we are to become masters. Do not expect, however, that God will infuse you with virtues without any effort on your part. Never believe that Father, Son, and Holy Spirit will simply flow into a person who has not been bent on acquiring virtue. Such virtue counts for very little unless it has been learned by intense effort, within as well as without.

There was once a farmer who fell into a state of rapture while threshing corn; if an Angel had not come and held the flail, he would have certainly struck himself. And yet you are asking forever to be given free time for contemplation, or at least this is what you say. And yet there is a lot of laziness in this. Everyone wants to be an eye; all want to contemplate and no one wants to perform the work.

I know a man much favored by God's grace: All his days he has been a ploughman. He has followed the plough for forty years, and that is what he does to this day. He once asked Our Lord whether he should give up work and go and sit in church. The answer was: No, He did not want that. He wanted him to go on earning his bread with the sweat of his brow to the honor of His Most Precious Blood.

A man ought to find some suitable time, during the day or night, to sink into his depth, each according to his own fashion. Let those noble creatures who are wholly steeped in God, without the aid of sensible images, do that; that is their way. And let the others do whatever suits them best, spending a good hour in spiritual exercises, each according to his own fashion, for we cannot all be eyes and give ourselves up to contemplation.

Let them devote themselves to those spiritual exercises to which they have been called, and let them do this with deep love, in peace and purity of heart, according to God's wish. When we serve God according to His will, we shall receive an answer according to our own will. But if we serve Him according to our own human will, God will not answer according to our own, but according to His, God's will.

From such self-denial is born an essential peace, the fruit of all our exercises of virtue. You may be sure that a peace which does not grow out of this is a false peace. It must be practiced actively and passively: The peace that arises from your interior life, no one will be able to take from you.

Along come the conceited people with their pretensions: They have their own theories, and they want to judge everyone accordingly. Forty years they have spent in the religious life and they still do not know what they are about. They are much bolder than I am. I have been called to teach, but when I listen to such people I wonder in what state they are and how they arrive at their conclusions. But even then I do not pass judgment, and I turn to Our Lord; and if I fail to receive an answer, I say to them: "My dear people, address yourselves to the Lord! He will judge you aright." You, however, wish to assign a place to everyone and judge them according to your private opinions.

Now the worms begin to eat away at the tender plant that was meant to grow in God's garden. And those others will say: "This is not the customary way, it must be some new fad and it smacks of novelty." What they forget is that God's ways are mysterious and hidden to them. How surprised will they, who are so sure of themselves now, be on the Day of Judgment!

Saint Paul teaches that it is the Spirit Who bestows the gift of discerning knowledge. Who, do you think, are the people on whom God has conferred that gift? You may be certain that they are those far advanced in the spiritual life, so far that it pervades their very being. They have withstood the most terrifying and severe temptations as well as the attacks of the Evil One, attacks so fierce that they shook them through bone and marrow. These are the people who possess the gift of discerning knowledge. If they want to avail themselves of this gift and observe others, they recognize right away whether it is God's Spirit that is at work in them, which path will lead to their sanctification and what may hinder their progress.

Alas, we forfeit truth in such a pernicious way; and we do this for the sake of such trivialities. As a result we incur the loss of the most sublime truth now and forever, throughout God's eternity. What we neglect now will never be ours.

May God help us to perform the work to which his Spirit has called us, each according to the revelation he has received.

AMEN.

SERMON 55

[FEAST OF OUR LADY'S NATIVITY]

Transite ad me omnes qui concupiscitis me et a generacionibus
meis adinplemini
Come all to me who desire me, and be sated by my fruits
(Wis 24:19)

> This Sermon, preached on the feast of Our Lady's Birth-
> day, points to her as a model, and urges us to ardently as-
> pire to the divine birth in us.

Today we celebrate the lovely feast on which the blessed Virgin, Our Lady, was born, free from sin, immaculate and holy from her mother's womb, in which she had been sanctified. In her was restored what had been lost in Paradise—that noble image which the Father had fashioned after his likeness and which was destroyed by sin. She has, together with the Father, given new life to all members of the Mystical Body, by guiding them back to their origin. Out of His unfathomable mercy God willed to rescue us with her aid from the everylasting abyss into which, for our own part, we would have fallen. Now it has been said about the Virgin in the Book of Wisdom: "Come all to me who desire me, and be sated by my fruits."

In the first instance these words are applied to the Heavenly Father, and they lead and draw us to the birth of the Son in eternity. But the same words Wisdom applied with equal propriety to the Virgin, for the birth which occurs within the Heavenly Father eternally was effected in her in time. And so she bids us to rise above ourselves, so that we, too, may be sated by the fruits of this wondrous birth. Holy Wisdom spoke: "All you who really desire me, and who desire this birth truly and genuinely, will at times be touched by a beam of its radiance." Thus our desire is made to surge upward and is caused to grow ever stronger.

Let us then say with Saint Augustine: "Lord, thou hast made us for Thyself, and our hearts are restless until they rest in Thee." This divine restlessness, which should always be ours, is smothered and dispelled by all kinds of alien forces generated in us: transitory, fleeting, and sensual things that come before our minds; inordinate affections for creatures, animate or inanimate; friendships, society, fashions, food; in short, everything which distracts us from our primary search for God. These divisive forces generate alien births in us, and as long as we deliberately consent to them, however trivial and petty they may seem, the divine birth will not occur. Such trivialities deprive us of the most high God and of that wondrous birth He wishes to bring to pass in us. Moreover, they deaden desire for God and His birth and rob us of that splendid anticipation which we should cherish. Of such great things we are deprived by such trivial attachments.

And then people will come and complain: "Alas, I have no love and feel no longing for God!" Well, it all depends on you. Why do you allow earthly attachments to smother that love? Search your hearts and consider what obstacles come between you and God; after all, you know best. Do not ask me but ask yourselves why you are lacking in love and longing. If you wish to possess God and creatures both together, you are bound to fail. You cannot choose both, no matter how many tears of blood you may shed.

Here I do not refer to necessities, or to gifts we possess through and in God, or such things that human nature cannot do without. When we are hungry and thirsty we will naturally enjoy food and drink, and when tired and weary, we will look forward to rest and sleep. If, however, we are motivated by sheer greed instead of using these things for our natural good, then they, too, may prove to be stumbling blocks to the birth of God in us, although it must be said that there are many more harmful pleasures than these. For we must remember that it is not always possible to distinguish between the necessities demanded by nature and the pleasure which satisfies these necessities.

That person, however, who does not wish to thwart the eternal birth, but wishes to progress in holy desire, should keep a watchful eye on the pleasures of the senses, of human nature, and of created things. The fewer the obstacles, the greater will be the desire [for

God's birth]. If heat is to enter, cold must necessarily go out. Also, one should not give way to complacency and carelessness, to love of comfort or any other blind weakness.

And yet, so many people will go through life as if blind, acting rashly, unreasonably, and without foresight. You may be sure that no confessor has any power over all these failings rooted in worldly attachments and in spiritual indifference, not as long as you willingly persevere in them; even if you confessed them ten times a day it would be to no avail, unless you were willing to rectify your intentions.

And furthermore, should you be found at the hour of death consciously adhering to worldly concerns, you will not enter into the presence of God. The whole of Scripture dwells on this theme, and the Gospels are imbued with it; it is the mandate of both the Old and the New Testament that one must love God totally, with all one's mind and heart.

We read in the Gospels: "Anyone who does not renounce all his possessions is not worthy of Me." We also read: "Not everyone who says 'Lord, Lord' will enter the Kingdom of Heaven, but those who do the will of my Father." Do you believe that God wishes to share His Kingdom with such unworthy creatures who reject Him, and that it was for them that He shed His precious blood and gave His life? Be on your guard! God will not look on forever. If you could conceive the fierceness of divine wrath, you would tremble with terror. God has given us all things in order that they may lead us to Him; He alone is to be the purpose of our lives, our sole destiny. Do you believe God can be mocked? No indeed. Belonging to a religious order does not convey holiness, nor does any cowl or any tonsure, any cloister or any community. More than this is required. I must have a holy, unattached, pure ground within myself, should I ever achieve holiness.

Holiness does not consist in exclaiming "Lord, Lord," or in reciting a lot of prayers, reading fine books, and impressing the world with my brilliance and eloquence. Something more radical is needed. And if you deceive yourselves about this, you only have yourselves to blame. Look at your worldly heart and disposition, your general unworthiness in spite of your religious habit, and see if all this cannot be compared to a gardener who grafts an alien shoot to a tree; the fruits that stem from it resemble the graft of the alien shoot, and not those of the tree. In the same way your good works, which ought to be of God, remain works of the world and therefore useless, for they grow out of your own creatureliness.

In regard to this, Job says: "In the horror of a vision by night, when deep sleep is wont to hold men, fear seized upon me and trembling, and all my bones were affrighted. And when the spirit passed before me, the hair of my flesh stood up." This horror of the nocturnal judgment is the dark and blind taking possession of the heart by creatures, and it is followed by an inexpressible dread and shuddering that make one's bones tremble. The passing of the spirit is the passing by of God.

Now the Gospels, too, speak of a "*transitus*," a passage. The word "*transite*" is used twice and stands for a twofold passing; the first passing of the spirit means God's passage toward us, the second our passage toward God. For this to happen, there must first be an exit, because, as the masters tells us, one thing cannot have two forms. The wood must first burn down if the fire is to blaze; the seeds must die if the tree is to grow; if God is to penetrate our innermost core to bring to pass His birth in us, then our creaturely selves must be brought to nothing.

Concerning the passage "the hair of my flesh stood up when a spirit passed before me," Saint Gregory refers to the Levites, who had to be shorn of their hair. Just as hair has its roots in the flesh, so is our attachment to created things in the lower and higher faculties rooted in our former habits. These must be shorn off with the sharp shears of holy fervor. The shears one should sharpen against the grindstone of God's fierce, all-powerful, and hidden judgment and against His swift justice, from which not one of our thoughts is hidden. For the most trifling image to which we willingly adhere, we shall have to suffer unbearable purgatorial pain before we attain to God's presence.

But no sooner has this hair been shorn off than it grows back again, and the sharp shears must attack it with renewed fervor. There are people who exercise such iron discipline over their thoughts that they reject them as soon as they are aware of them. Such control is laboriously cultivated, but once the habit has been established, it comes quite easily. And what initially required an iron will can now be disposed of with a flick of the wrist.

Furthermore, you should be filled with an active and universal love, not merely for those of your own kind, but for all men—no matter whether they are virtuous or not—and particularly for the poor, without excluding anyone. Such was the love expressed by Our Lady's parents, who were so much beloved by God. They divided all their belongings into three parts: One was set aside for the service of God and the Temple, the second for the poor, and the third part they used for their own livelihood. You may be certain that wherever a tendency toward gluttony and greed dominates, there exists a foul and filthy ground throughout. We should rid ourselves of such worthless and transitory things with great eagerness. Whoever gives will receive, who forgives will be forgiven, and with what measure you mete out, it will be returned to you again.

However, some people cling to hidden attachments of which they are generally unaware, and these, too, produce growth of evil hair. These false and hidden motives could prevent them from entering God's presence. Such people may indeed have led exemplary lives and excelled in exercises of great piety, but that to which they cleave and cling lies so deeply buried that they are not even conscious of it. Therefore it would be of advantage to those who genuinely wish to live the truth to be directed by an experienced friend of God who will guide them according to God's ways. For these false and hidden tendencies are not so easily detected, and it takes experience with similar cases to discern them. Such people should search far and wide to find an experienced friend of God who can lead them in the right direction. Should this be impossible, an ordinary confessor would be sufficient; he may be a simple man, but the Holy Spirit will nevertheless speak through him by virtue of his office, though he may not be learned. One ought to submit to his judgment, take his advice, and not wish to live according to one's own counsel.

In regard to this we possess a perfect model in the holy Virgin. When still a child, she obeyed her elders, her father and mother, after which she was placed under the guidance of the priest at the Temple; later she was under the protection of Saint Joseph, and finally under the care of Our Lord Jesus Christ, who then commended her to Saint John.

And hence we wish to ask her today most devoutly that she may take us also under her care and that she may deliver us anew, on her birthday, into our true origin. May God help us to attain this.

AMEN.

SERMON 59

[EXALTATION OF THE CROSS II]

Ego si exaltatus fuero, omnia traham ad me ipsum
If I be lifted up, I will draw all things to Myself (Jn 12:32)

After a brief introduction to the Feast of the Exaltation of
the holy Cross, this Sermon teaches how to lift up the
Cross within us so that the Lord may draw us to Himself.
It also teaches how our venial sins can become an occasion
for comprehending our own nothingness and how we may
enter into the hiddenness of the divine abyss after having
overcome our two lower natures.

Today is the feast of the exaltation of the most precious and holy
Cross. It is a sheer impossibility to express in words its dignity,
for it contains within itself all honor and glory that the human mind
can conceive, in time and in eternity. For in the Cross we see Him
who died upon it. It is for this reason that religious of every order
take up the Cross on this day and begin the fast according to their
rule. It is a wholesome thing for those capable of it, and a joyful one
as well.

We observe today the occasion on which a Christian Emperor
rescued the Holy Cross from a pagan king and returned it to Jerusalem with all the honor and dignity which he, a ruler, could show
to his own glory rather than to that of the Cross. But when he rode
up to the city, the gates barred his entrance and closed before him,
forming a strong and mighty wall. An Angel was stationed there and
said: "You come riding up in all your majesty, bringing the Cross.
He, however, who died upon it was driven out of this city in bitter
shame and disgrace, walking barefoot and carrying the Cross on His
shoulders." The Emperor dismounted at once, stripped off his shirt,

and took the Cross on his shoulders, whereupon the gates flew open and he carried it into the city. Many signs and wonders were observed when the sick and the lame, the blind and the crippled were cured.

Our Lord said: "If I am lifted up, I shall draw all things to myself." Here He refers to man who bears a likeness to all created things. There are many who find the Cross by means of much suffering and numerous trials, and this is the way God draws them to Himself. But this suffering must not be merely encountered, it must be lifted up, exalted, as it is on today's feast. If we looked into our hearts we would find the Cross there twenty times a day in many painful incidents and afflictions by which we are indeed crucified if only we understood the sign. Instead we try to avoid taking up the Cross, and that way we commit a grave injustice. One should assume that burden freely, lift it right up to God, and then accept it as one's very own, be the circumstances external or internal, corporal or spiritual. Thus one is drawn into God, into Him who will draw all things to Himself, as He said He would now that He is lifted up.

We meet people who do indeed carry the Cross outwardly, performing good and pious exercises and having taken upon themselves the burden of monastic life. They do a lot of chanting and reading, they take their place in choir and in the refectory, but they do our Lord a minor service because they are only externally involved. Do you suppose God has created you like so many songbirds? You were to be his beloved brides and spouses. Such people carry the Cross in an outward manner, but they are extremely careful that it does not touch them too closely, and they try to avoid it whenever they can. Instead of carrying it freely, they have it forced upon them, like Simon the Cyrenian. However, even in this there is some benefit, for it protects against vice and frivolity and it saves from the terrible pains of purgatory, perhaps even from eternal damnation itself.

"I will draw all things to myself," Our Lord said. Now, if one wishes to draw things, one must first gather them together. This is precisely what Our Lord does. He calls us back from our vagaries and distractions, our external business, the use of our senses, and faculties, words, and actions. He calls us back from our interior preoccupations and opinions, our phantasies and desires, our inclinations and perceptions, our willing and our love. And once all these forces have been gathered up, God draws us to Himself, but only after all our attachments have been shed. This whole process is indeed a heavy Cross, all the heavier in proportion to our attachments. For we must rid outselves of the pleasure and love we have in created things, no matter how godly or holy they may seem, if we are to be truly exalted and drawn into God.

This is the first and lowest stage, when we have to strip ourselves of everything. This taking up of the Cross concerns the outward life. After this, however, the same process has to be repeated inwardly. Here we must renounce interior delight, all spiritual attachments and joys, even those which are the results of our acts of virtue. The scholars have learned debates whether one ought to take delight in acts of virtue or whether one should simply perform them for their usefulness; delight is reserved for God alone. Yet, how can one practice virtue without delighting in it? What one ought to do is practice it and forget oneself in the process.

Beloved! What do you think delight and satisfaction really are? That I can fast, keep vigils, pray, observe the Rule of my order? That I should find great self-fulfillment in these was hardly God's intention. Why, do you believe, does God barely allow one day or one night to be like the next? What aided your devotion yesterday is no help whatever today. Today your mind is filled with a great number of images and distractions, and nothing comes of your devotions.

Accept this cross from God and bear it in the depth of your heart. What a very sweet cross it would become if you offered it to God in loving surrender and gratitude. "My soul does magnify the Lord and exalts God's greatness in all things." No matter whether He gives or takes away, the Son of man is to be exalted on the Cross. Our sisters have purified the depth of their souls but they are still too much attached [to things], too anxious to feel and taste God and to comprehend Him rationally. Dear sisters, leave all that. Strive instead for true abandonment, be sober, and consider yourselves unworthy of such great favors. Remember to find the Cross in trials and temptations rather than in the full bloom of sentimental emotion. For we must always continue to carry the Cross.

"Christ had to suffer these things to enter into His glory." Whatever light or joy may be yours, do not be overly concerned with it. Instead, sink unquestioningly into your own nothingness, be conscious of your nothingness and cling to this, to nothing else. Our Lord said: "If any man will come after me, let him deny himself, take up his Cross, and follow me." It is not by high emotions but by the Cross that we follow God. Thus our dear Saint Andrew greeted the

Cross with these words: "Hail holy Cross, how I have longed for you with all my heart. Remove me from this world and make me one with my Lord." And such a disposition must be a constant one. Without interruption you should search yourselves, both within and without. Make an accounting of your sins and failings, and if you fall seventy times a day, rise seventy times and return to God so that you will not fall too often. Hasten to Him and fervently beseech Him to rid you of your sins swiftly, so that you will have forgotten them by the time you reach the confessional. Do not let the tendency to sin overwhelm you. For it is to help, not to hurt, that God permits it. It should lead you to the knowledge of your own nothingness and to deep humility, without, however, resulting in despondence. What matters is a good and ready will to obey God. No one is born free from sin as Our Lady was. Hence you should be well pleased to take both the suffering and the Cross upon you. As Saint Paul said: "All things work together for good to them that love God." And the exegesis adds: "Be silent and flee to God; consider your nothingness, remain in yourself, and do not go to your confessor after every small fault."

Saint Matthew followed the Lord the moment he was called, without instruction or preparation. If you find yourself falling short, make not too much of this cross; let rather divine truth measure it out, and show contrition in your heart. Not those who are in Christ will be condemned but those who willfully turn to created things in His stead. To them who love God with mind and heart, this cross works all for the good. But one thing I would like to tell you in all frankness: If you allow creatures to absorb you, and that with your full consent, and if you seek occasions of sin, then it will work toward your condemnation. Even if God granted you the gift of repentance—which is very uncertain—you will suffer bitter purgatorial pains; so bitter that you could not bear the thought of it now. And furthermore, should you receive the Body of Our Lord in this state—and this is what a great saint has said—"it would be like pushing a delicate child into a filthy cesspool." This is the way you treat the living Son of God who gave himself up for you out of love. And finally, if you go to confession without having freely resolved to avoid the occasions of sin, the Pope with all his Cardinals could not absolve you because you are lacking true repentance. Remember that each time you do this you become guilty of the Body of Our Lord.

Our Lord has said: "If any man come after me, let him deny himself, take up his cross, and follow me." This act of self-denial is taken so seriously by many a devout friend of God that one hardly dares to say in what a radical manner one has to go about it, in whatever state of life one finds oneself. What costs little is worth little, and who sows sparingly will reap sparingly. How you measure out, so it will be measured to you. However, let all this rest with God.

Yet, what is the purpose of all my talking if you cling to your old ways, and believe only in the effectiveness of external devotions of your own choice? Give yourself up to the Lord and die to your own self completely. The Lord has said: "Follow me!" The servant always follows his master, he does not go before him. He does not act according to his will but according to that of his master. We can observe how such obedience is carried out even in the world where all time and diligence, strength and will are at the service of one's master.

My Beloved! The grain of wheat must die before it can bring forth fruit; and so, you too must die utterly to your will. Only to God should you offer your will and your surrender, and in such a way as if you had never possessed a will of your own.

Once a devout nun stood singing in choir and prayed: "Lord, this time is yours and mine. But if I turn inward, it is yours and not mine." If a man wishes to surrender himself to God, he should first rid himself, in a spiritual way, of every trace of self-will. Man is in a certain sense three men: an animal man who lives according to his senses, a rational man, and finally the highest man in the form of God, deiform. It is on this highest level that we should turn to God and, prostrate before the divine abyss, abandon ourselves completely and become captives of divine love. We must rise above our lower natures and keep them in check. Saint Bernard has this to say on the subject: "The effort it requires to withdraw the sensual part of ourselves with all its lusts from the things to which it was attached—and what a heavy cross that is, you know very well—is no greater than the effort needed to draw the exterior self inward, from the visible world to the invisible." Essentially this process leads to what Augustine calls "*abditum mentis*," the spirit's secret hiding place.

Let us accept as a God-given cross all the incidents and trials that afflict our two lower natures, even when they appear as hindrances to our turning toward God. Let us commend them to Him, no matter whether they are sensual or rational concerns. Let us gladly leave them behind.

Now we should rise with all our might into our highest nature. This is what Abraham did when he left his servant and his ass at the foot of the mountain and went up alone with his son. In the same manner you should leave the ass, your animal man [and what an ass he is!] behind and do the same with the servant, your natural reason, which is meant to serve you. They have done their duty; leave them both behind. They have brought you to the foot of the mountain, the ascent to God: There they should stay. Leaving them there, you must start the ascent with your son, that is, with your mind and heart toward that secret place, the Holy of Holies, to offer your sacrifice there. Give yourself entirely to God, enter, and hide the hidden ground of your spirit, as Augustine calls it, in the hiddenness of the divine abyss. Thus the Prophet says in the Psalms: "Lord, you will hide them in the hiddenness of your countenance." In this hiddenness the created spirit is borne back into the uncreated state in which it dwelt from all eternity. There it knows itself in God, raised to a divine level, and in its creaturehood it sees itself a created being. But in God all things which participate in this ground are God. "When a man enters here," says Proclus, "he is unaware of anything that may happen to him, be it poverty, sickness, or suffering of any kind."

The Prophet speaks: "Lord, you will protect them from the afflictions of men." These souls now follow the Lord according to His Words: "I am in the Father, and the Father in me; likewise, I am in you and you are in Me."

May we be drawn into Our Lord the way He wished to draw all things to Himself. May we take up the Cross in such a way that we enter the true ground where He has gone before us, He who died for all on the Cross. May God grant this.

AMEN.

SERMON 76
[TWENTY-SECOND SUNDAY AFTER TRINITY]

Oro, fratres, ut caritas vestra magis ac magis abundet . . .
And this is my prayer for you;
may your love grow richer and richer yet . . .(Phil 1,9)

This Sermon deals with Saint Paul's text for the Twenty-second Sunday after Trinity in which he speaks of the full harvest of love. We are instructed to bear patiently with the failings of our neighbor and to submit ourselves and all our desires to the loving will of God.

Saint Paul says: "May your love grow richer and richer yet," and more precisely: "God knows how I long for you all, with the tenderness of Jesus Christ Himself, and this is my prayer for you; may your love grow richer and richer yet, in the fullness of its knowledge and the depth of its perception, so that you may learn to prize what is of value; may nothing cloud your consciences or hinder your progress till the day when Christ comes; may you reap, through Jesus Christ, the full harvest of your justification to God's glory and praise." With intense emotion Saint Paul tells us that God is his witness how close to his heart are his own. If we only had love, we should be profoundly moved by the radical demands God's friends make on us. If we had no other reason, this would be reason enough to abide by their wishes. Saint Paul says: "May your love grow richer and richer yet," he prays that our imperfect love may grow into a perfect one.

The noblest and most precious thing one can speak of is love. Nothing else could be more salutary. It is not great learning or high thoughts that God asks of us, nor does He demand a lot of external devotions—though they have their place. It is love and love alone which ennobles such practices. God desires nothing else but love, for, as Saint Paul puts it, love is the bond of perfection. Do not Jews and pagans display great gifts of mind? The just as well as the unjust perform good works, but love alone separates the good from the bad. For God is love, and those who dwell in love dwell in Him and He in them. This is reason enough why we should learn all about true love. Saint Augustine had this in mind when he said: "Since God loved us first so immeasurably, we should certainly love Him in return." That way our love can never be wasted nor can it ever diminish; on the contrary, it waxes and grows ever more, for love deserves love, and the greater one loves the greater one is enabled to love.

Love has two manifestations: an interior and an exterior one. The exterior one is directed toward one's neighbor, the interior one toward God. The right exercise of love requires understanding; Saint Paul speaks of the fullness of its knowledge and the depth of its perception. We should become overflowing with love. Knowledge is the third gift of the Holy Spirit and it precedes love, such as a handmaid who serves a noble woman will precede her.

True divine love, which you must nourish within yourself, can be recognized by the love you bear your neighbor. For it has been written: "How can you love God, Whom you have not seen, and not love your neighbor whom you see?" All the divine commandments and counsels derive from this one source: "Love God and your neighbor as you love yourself." You should rejoice and suffer with him, be of one mind and heart, as it was in the days of the Apostles: "They shared everything with each other." If you are unable to put this into practice because of the circumstances of your life, then you should express it by an interior disposition, grounded in truth, purity of intention, affection, and love. If you cannot do anything for your neighbor, then say a good and generous word to him, one that arises from the depth of a good and honest heart.

Your love must embrace also those who suffer from numerous shortcomings. Their faults should be borne with gentle patience and with much love. Do not sit in judgment upon them but bear patiently whatever it is they may harbor against you. Sometimes their unseemly conduct does not arise from any malice but merely from thoughtlessness or indolence, or, as Saint Gregory puts it, because God has seen fit to bring them low so that they might become aware of their faults. Such people, whose failings are not caused by vicious habits but by exterior circumstances, often make a turnabout, condemn themselves, and admit their guilt. They are very different from others, who remain obstinate and will never acknowledge their faults. Show forbearance to all of these and consider this a test of your love. But if you fall upon them with harsh judgments, hotheadedly, you may be sure that divine love has grown cold and will further diminish in you.

My dear Sisters, such a disposition would indeed be worthy of love. Whoever could bring about such a reversal at his last hour and be found wholly submerged in God's holy will, he would come to God without hindrance, no matter how many sins he may have committed during his life. But this is a grace God alone can confer. To die in such a state would be good and holy; to live in it, noble and salutary. Such souls reap a wondrous harvest without ceasing: Love becomes immersed in the Beloved.

Nevertheless, sin remains love's adversary. Grave and serious temptation will strike in all possible disguises. Listen to me carefully: Temptation as temptation, as a grave inroad of sin, must by all means be rejected. Not, however, the purifying pain one must undergo in order to overcome it. It is a heavy yoke indeed, and it ought to be readily accepted. If it were God's wish that a man were to endure this pain until the Day of Judgment, he should endure it gladly, to God's glory and praise. And should God choose to bestow this hard-won reward upon another person, be it a pagan, or a Jew, or a man across the oceans whom you have never seen, then, according to God's will, you should wish him well from the very depth of your heart.

Love meets more adversaries on the way. It wishes to savor the Beloved, rejoice in Him in sweet delectation. Nevertheless, if God should choose to withdraw this joy at the very moment of its fulfillment and grant it to your greatest enemy, you should not begrudge it but offer it to him gladly out of the goodness of your heart.

I once knew a friend of God, a very holy man, who said that he desired his neighbor's eternal bliss more ardently than his own. This to him was the meaning of true love. The objects of a loving man's desire are so various: He might long for poverty or whatever. Would it not be better to commend your entire life to love? Go out of yourself in self-surrender, free yourself of all attachments in humility and singleness of mind. Where love is concerned, one should show abundant insight and strive for ever greater understanding so that one may possess it not merely in a good but in the very best way, always mindful of its right exercise, for the enemy has sown weeds amongst the roses so that they may be stifled. It is true that you must avoid certain persons, act differently from them, be it in religious life or in the world. A friend of God must conduct himself differently from a friend of the world, but this should not imply a separation from one's neighbor.

This love of which Saint Paul says that it should grow richer and richer yet has left traces in the lower faculties as well. From it human nature derives spiritual sweetness, tidbits and delicious wine. The disciples of Our Lord partook of this love when He still dwelt amongst them. And yet He said to them: "It is good for you that I shall go from you" [he referred to His physical presence]. Should the disciples receive Him in a spiritual manner, He would have to leave them according to the flesh.

Now I will speak of another love, and it is as high above the first as Heaven is above earth. It was experienced by the Apostles after the Ascension. Whoever could attain to this love would have attained a lofty peak indeed. Here the self is left far behind; and instead of fullness there is emptiness. Not Knowledge, but non-Knowledge prevails now; for that love is beyond all modes and manners. Oh, what great pain this causes our poor human nature, which is now twisting and turning like a child deprived of its mother's breast. Angry nature with its nooks and corners is totally lost because this new love transcends its power and effectiveness. So entirely stripped must it be of self that this very self eludes its glance. Neither thought nor desire can it harbor. It cannot even sacrifice this poverty to God, for in its non-Knowledge it cleaves closely to it. It must deny its very self, and die to all sensible images which it possessed in the first stage, in order to enter that realm where God loves Himself and is His own object of love. In this denuding of ourselves we are reformed in the form of God, clothed with His divinity. It is the hidden darkness of which Saint Dionysius spoke. Now our poor nature is led along another path, tempted not only inwardly but also outwardly, bare of every support or comfort. The Body of Our Lord, of which it partook daily, is now withdrawn according to God's ordinance. It enters upon another path, way above itself, where the spirit rests in God's Spirit, in the secret silence of the divine Essence. Here the light shines in the darkness, and the simple essence is comprehended by itself and in itself. Here all differentiation [in regard to God] gives way to unity. It is the day of Jesus Christ of which Saint Paul spoke. It is the true day on which is truly received the harvest of His Passion and death. It is the radiant day of Redemption. Not that the suffering and death of Our Lord would not have been experienced with greater purity in Himself; but in us they are now received in a loftier manner, devoid of sensible images, beheld from within in a sublime, exalted and mysterious manner, quite different from what we had experienced before.

Let me elucidate this by way of comparison. Before His death Our Lord allowed Himself to be touched and anointed by Mary Magdalene. But after He entered into His immortal state He said to her: "Do not touch me for I have not yet ascended to the Father." In the first stage, the lowest one, He permitted her to wash His feet and to anoint Him in a bodily way; in the higher stage He allowed this only in a spiritual way, as He exists in the Father. Here is enacted that glorious spectacle in which the Son returns the love He has received from the Father, and both—in a burst of love—breathe forth the Holy Spirit. This is the true day on which true love is born in true nobility through Jesus Christ, as Saint Gregory writes: "*Per dominum Iesum Christum.*" A member of our Order, addressing our Chapter, has put it this way: "The light of Jesus Christ illuminates our souls more radiantly than all the suns of the universe, sending its rays from the inside out." My beloved Sisters! Here is an increase beyond measure, not only every day, but every hour and every minute. Let us reflect upon ourselves and contemplate seriously this life of love. This is what the true friends of God desire earnestly, and hence Saint Paul prays that our love may grow richer and richer yet.

May He, Who is true love, enable us to experience it fully.

AMEN.

INDEX TO INTRODUCTION

INDEX

INDEX TO TEXTS

INDEX

INDEX

Humility, 65, 81, 117–19;
    child's, 44; complacency
    contrasted, 53; necessity,
    47, 108, 124; sin and, 132,
    166; witness and, 77
Hunger for God, 159
Hunting analogy, 56–57

Images of God, 104, 126; soul
    as, 128
Immaculate Conception, 158
Impetuosity, *see* Rashness
Impurity, 42, 86
Inertia, 112
Intellect, 89, 105
Introversion, need for, 37
Inwardness, 125–27, 147–48;
    Holy Spirit and, 80, 85,
    92–93, 106; necessity of,
    106, 107
Israel, symbolism of, 43

James, St., 62
Jeremiah, 63, 65, 66
Jerome, St., 99
Jesus, 104, 107, 138, 139; birth,
    35, 36; generation, 36;
    Good Shepherd, as, 98–
    102; Mystical Body, 140,
    154; Passion, 74; teaching
    methods, 82
Job, 161
Joel, 102
John the Baptist, St., 145, 150–
    51
John the Evangelist, St., 148
Joseph, St., 41–43
Jubilation, 58, 141, 142
Judgmental attitudes, *see* Self-
    righteousness

Kin, sensory pleasures as, 38
Knowledge, 94–95, 106, 107,
    171

Lenten sermons, 50–61
Levites, 161
Light: Christ as, 50, 53; Holy
    Spirit and, 81; human
    nature and, 35; reason and,
    52; self-will and, 52; source
    of, 50; witness to, 145–46
Living water, 63–65, 66
Love, 169–73; capacity for, 131;
    inordinate, 69, 111; light
    and, 149; nobility of, 160–
    70, 173; stages of, 149–50;
    temporal objects, 37
Love of God, 118–19, 125;
    Richard of St. Victor on,
    67; worldliness blocking,
    160
Love of neighbor, 132, 141;
    inordinate, 69; universal,
    161–62, 170–71; work and,
    154, 155
Luxury, 111

Malice, 42
Martha, 155
Martyrs, 95
Mary, mother of Jesus, 35, 39–
    40; Immaculate
    Conception, 158;
    obedience, 162
Mary Magdalene, 173
Matthew, St., 166
Measures of grain, 130
Medicines, excessive, 87
Meekness, 124
Memory, 37, 105

INDEX

INDEX

INDEX

Other Volumes in this Series